Chaos AND Quietness

Chaos and Quietness

Discovering Fall's Cleansing,
Winter's Comfort, Spring's Hope,
and a Summer Purpose

Cynthia Hartson Ross

XULON PRESS

Xulon Press
2301 Lucien Way #415
Maitland, FL 32751
407.339.4217
www.xulonpress.com

© 2021 by Cynthia Hartson Ross
www.ablessingofbeauty.com

All rights reserved solely by the author. The author guarantees all contents are original and do not infringe upon the legal rights of any other person or work. No part of this book may be reproduced in any form without the permission of the author. The views expressed in this book are not necessarily those of the publisher.
Due to the changing nature of the Internet, if there are any web addresses, links, or URLs included in this manuscript, these may have been altered and may no longer be accessible. The views and opinions shared in this book belong solely to the author and do not necessarily reflect those of the publisher. The publisher, therefore, disclaims responsibility for the views or opinions expressed within the work.

Unless otherwise indicated, Scripture quotations taken from the King James Version (KJV) – *public domain.*
Scripture quotations taken from the Holy Bible, New International Version (NIV). Copyright © 1973, 1978, 1984, 2011 by Biblica, Inc.™. Used by permission. All rights reserved.
Scripture quotations taken from The Message (MSG). Copyright © 1993, 1994, 1995, 1996, 2000, 2001, 2002. Used by permission of NavPress Publishing Group. Used by permission. All rights reserved.
Scripture quotations taken from the Holy Bible, New Living Translation (NLT). Copyright ©1996, 2004, 2007 by Tyndale House Foundation. Used by permission of Tyndale House Publishers, Inc.
Scripture quotations taken from the New King James Version (NKJV). Copyright © 1982 by Thomas Nelson, Inc. Used by permission. All rights reserved.

Names in some anecdotes and stories have been changed to protect the identities of the persons involved.

Paperback ISBN-13: 978-1-66283-298-7
Ebook ISBN-13: 978-1-66283-299-4

Table of Contents

Preface vii
The Author's Chaos. xi

~ Fall ~

Chaos & Quietness of Fall 1
   Visible Signs 2
   A Deep Personal Cleansing. 6
   Cleansing for Root Health. 7
   A Good Pruning. 9
   Intentional Wounds 11
   Intentional Healing 11
   Fall and Forgiveness 13
   Past Failures 14
   Encouragement time! 15
   Carry A Burden. 17
   My Own Unnecessary Wounding 19
   Living for Christ In a PC World 22
   Story Time 24
   Quiet Chaos. 25

~Winter~

Chaos & Quietness of Winter 33
   Winter Rest 37
   Distractions. 40
   Creating Storms of Chaos 42

Purpose in Chaos 43
Rest Needs Supervision 44
After The Struggle. 49
For His Good Pleasure 50

~Spring~

Chaos & Quietness of Spring 52
    Hard Questions 56
    HOPE 58
    The Process 60
    Spring-Loading Spring 61
    The Analysis 63
    Equip His Saints? 69
    Storm Cycles. 72

~Summer~

Chaos & Quietness of Summer. 77
    Express Yourself 79
    Sneaks Up 83
    Story Time 88

The Invitation 96

Dedication. 100

About the Author. 103

Preface

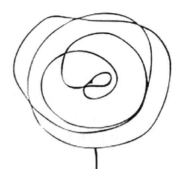

"...a delicate whispering voice..."
(1 Kings 19:11-13 NKJV)

It is as important to find peace in your chaos as it is to find the chaos that is stealing your peace. Perhaps, if your chaos is like mine, it is that tricky quiet chaos. The kind that just sneaks up on your soul-refreshing moments and steals the peace right out of them. This kind of chaos requires patience, faith, and hope before the uncomplicated purpose for the cycle is revealed.

Even though chaos affects people differently, we know when we are in a season of it. I'm guessing if you picked up a book with the word "chaos" in the title, you are probably experiencing some version of it yourself right now? In this book, I will show you how chaos can be neutral, the villain, or the hero of your story. And—it is your choice!

Using metaphors from nature's seasons and cycles, I am offering you a chance to see chaos as an essential part of a faith-building, courage-making process, rather than God's instrument of destruction or Satan's tool of distraction.

What if chaotic moments are allowed to stir up the soil of our life? Test our root systems, cause us rest, or whisk up emotions that lead us back to a fuller, hope-filled relationship with the original hope-maker Himself? Nature is an excellent reminder of God's promises.

Could that be God's intention for allowing chaos in the first place?

God whispers, and mountains crumble! That kind of chaos beckons for a different sort of perspective. It takes focused faith to remain confident on top of a crumbling mound, trusting you will be just fine when the dust settles. To live or lead well during those chaotic moments requires hope, surrender, renewal, and purpose. It may even involve repurposing past chaos.

It. Is. Possible.

I want to show you how to find deep comfort in a Winter's rest, inspiring hope in regenerative Spring, passion and purpose in expressive Summer, and great redemptive value in a painful Fall pruning or cleansing cycle. You'll learn to recognize your natural chaotic responses triggered by self or others and how to let that chaos lead you back to a quieting, mountain-moving kind of love in Christ through the seasons.

I designed this book to be a fun metaphoric read about natural and chaotic responses. I write word pictures to help open the eyes of your heart and sometimes just have a good laugh. But while I talk a lot about nature and seasons, I am not advocating Pantheism. I believe God created nature, Christ in his pre-incarnate form, the Word of God, and so I put my faith in the Creator, not the created. That makes me a Jesus girl. Let me just put that out there now because the rest of this book will make much more sense to you if you understand the compass I'm using for hope and navigating chaos.

I don't know if you only have faith enough for one last prayer or if you've never even heard about Jesus before, but everyone is welcome to this table. You will be fed. God has a plan, and you're in it, my friend. Christianity is based upon the nature of God. A display of that divine nature is His creation. But God is clear in his commands to worship the Creator, not the creation.

So while I use metaphorical seasonal examples in my storytelling, I do so to assist you in seeing the invisible qualities God has made plain since the creation of the world. I do this to call your attention back to the beauty and wonder of Christ-hope in your predictable and passing chaotic seasons.

None of us have to be alone in our chaos- none of us. There isn't a moment of chaos that hasn't been experienced by someone somewhere on this planet already. And while our chaotic experiences could feel very different from one another, the journey is something we all share in together; you, me, and the thousands who have come before, paving the roads with wisdom and their story.

So, may God cover your heart and mind as we travel wisely together. Making His Word our highest priority, we will slip back and forth between our creative, right-story-telling-brain and our left, logical-facts and Scripture brain. We need both to navigate these seasons of chaos and quietness together. I trust God will release what you genuinely need from our time together.

May God reveal more of himself to you today, my friend.

The Author's Chaos

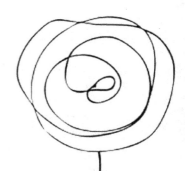

"Do not merely listen to the word, and so deceive yourselves. Do what it says." James 1:22

God Stands between my chaos and quietness.

The more chaos I have, the more time and help I need to understand it and make peace with it.

I'm in the midst of this incredibly chaotic creative process of writing. I'm standing at my desk, facing my whiteboard instead of sitting in my chair. I want to focus solely on what this book is meant to be for you and not me.

I've asked myself several times, if every human on the planet were gone, would I still go through the chaotic, mentally, and physically painful process of writing this book?

The answer is yes.

I am, without a doubt, called to write. Even if, for no other purpose than to be obedient to the calling, I will write. I will finish this book, and it will be in the timing perfect for each reader to receive a purposeful blessing.

I use a whiteboard as part of my creative process. I've been focusing on this whiteboard for the last 48 hours straight. I am trying to find the common thread that speaks into the chapters of this book and bring my so-called "season of rest" to closure; however, I'm unsettled about something, and I can't quite put my finger on it.

I'm so close to finishing, I can sense it, but I can't see it, so I stare, intensely looking for the missing piece (or peace).

Distraction calls. It's a sunny Saturday afternoon. My husband is out of town. I have the freedom to do whatever I please in these hours, yet here I stand, eyes blurred, neck stiff, stomach grumbling and joints inflamed. Yet, I'm focused with a hopeful purpose that comfort and rest will come once this chaotic but quiet obedience to my "season of rest" is completed.

My season of rest began when I heard the call to step away from full-time ministry responsibilities to pour into the life of my two grandchildren while I had the opportunity. My kids had been preparing to move eight states away very shortly, and of course, the grandbabies would be going with them. I had to reprioritize.

Now, the kids have gone, the house is quiet, and I have the freedom to write. But all I can feel on this mid-summer morning is the quiet chaos that fills the room. I close my eyes, breathe in deeply, lift my face and stretch my back. My body remains aching but stilled. One hand is clutching a dry erase marker, the other poised on the computer's keypad. I'm standing prepared to type the revelations I'm waiting for, and I'm intent upon receiving an answer of clarity.

The Author's Chaos

I send up a prayer and listen for a response. Then another, and still another. Nothing but silence in return. After what feels like hours of silent waiting, I decide to select some background music from my phone's playlist. I allow it to play on my senses artfully. The piano note's call me to dance with them, but I refuse. I am determined, stilled even until I've accomplished the goal for which I've come so far.

My prayers continue: Jesus, this messy, chaotic whiteboard must make sense today. Your message through me needs clarity, and I need real rest. This season of rest is exhausting me! I pray with a wrinkle in my brow and a deep exhale.

My senses are once again drawn to the beautiful piano notes swirling about the room. Suddenly, ever so faintly, amid this beautiful sonata, I hear the cry of what sounds like a newborn. Without disengaging from my prayers or opening my eyes, I listen more curiously and closely. Then, I hear it again.

Tilting my head from one side to the other, I question the cry of a newborn in the music of a master? Its unlikeliness should be chaotic to the melody, yet it draws me deeper into that stillness with Christ. My mind is released from its singular purpose and drawn into a peculiar and breathtakingly beautiful moment.

Eyes still closed, I whisper... *Where are you taking me, Lord?*

Then, the music stops. Complete silence again fills the room, but it is accompanied by an incredible sense of peace this time. I open my eyes. I gaze down at the iPhone that has been playing that hauntingly beautiful melody. Then, with eyes focused straight ahead, I look up at my whiteboard, fingers still clutching tightly to the colored dry erase markers and keypad. And then I see with childlike wonder the connection points to the message I am trying to deliver. It was as if the words upon the whiteboard had almost rearranged themselves.

I could see the space between chaos and quietness belonging solely to God and the cycles of nature reflecting God's perfect purpose:

- Fall as Cleansing Redemption and Reconciliation
- Winter as Comfort and Resting
- Spring as Hope and Regenerating
- Summer as Purpose and Radiating

I felt the blood rush back into my fingertips. Peace had finally arrived to neutralize the chaos of my season of rest. Peace entered my senses. Peace not from the art itself, but a peace that surpasses my complete understanding. Peace from obedience and surrender to a chaotically quiet writing process for God's good pleasure rather than my own.

My chaos is being repurposed for God's good pleasure as I create this artful, hope-filled work. God is revealing to me that this work will be used to assist the weary believer into a deeper, more purposeful relationship with Christ during quiet seasons or seasons of chaos in their own life.

But the beauty of how God is working through my season of quiet chaos and obedience is not over yet. He is teaching me to listen, really listen for His delicate whisper in the chaos.

Excited to dig into the writing now, I reach over and click replay on my iPhone. "Water Ripples" begins to play once again, and I begin to write. I listen for the sound of that newborn cry. But, no cry could be heard. I stop typing for a moment and turn back to my phone. I click replay again and then again. After several failed attempts at replaying that hauntingly beautiful melody that included the newborn cry, I realized the cry quite possibly may have been my own creative cry to Christ in those final chaotically quiet moments of obedience.

Or perhaps more likely, the neighbor's newborn letting out a timely squeal from across the quiet street? Who knows? All I know for sure is that I was obedient to stand firm, patiently waiting until I heard an answer. God was teaching me to lean into and not shy away from the discomfort of the task. I had to wait for the right words to be delivered at the right time, in faith, no matter how quiet or chaotic the season of obedience became.

And the answers came. Tasked with artfully writing "story" in a way that will speak His message of love to whoever they are written for, I write.

Perhaps For You!

It could be you are about to discover the peace in your chaos with childlike wonder and how to repurpose the chaos that has been stealing your peace.

I pray these stories will encourage you to do what you were born to do just the way you were born to do it- on purpose.

*C*ynthia Hartson Ross

~ Fall ~

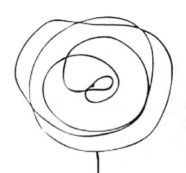

Chaos & Quietness of Fall

> "And we urge you, brothers, admonish the idle, encourage the fainthearted, help the weak, be patient with them all."
>
> 1 Thessalonians 5:14, ESV

Cleansing / Redemption

My hope is that by the end of this first chapter, you'll have found a fresh perspective on chaos and quietness, along with new tools that will enable you to see and experience hope, comfort, beauty, and purpose through every season of your life.

Seasons are in constant motion so that we can find ourselves full circle, lessons learned, and ready to reengage four seasons later. So I'm choosing to start you in Fall with a metaphoric word picture that will offer you a whimsical yet practical interpretation of a Fall "cleansing" cycle. In this season, we can also better relate and appreciate a purposeful life's "pruning" by the hand of God himself.

We are using a fruit-bearing tree as our first metaphor. This is going to make sense as it comes to life with the colors of your own circumstances. Symbolically, fruit is a sign of life both spiritually and metaphorically. We are talking about the process of producing a fruitful life that requires cycles of cutting back to grow forward. Keep that in mind as we head into Fall.

Cleansing and pruning are very different from one another, yet both are most prevalent in nature's Fall cycle, and both will require periods of quiet recovery. Both are necessary experiences for continued healthy growth cycles in a fruit-bearing tree. Cleansing tends to stir things up a bit; it also is the process by which the elimination of unnecessary toxic connections are being cycled. In addition, it takes energy to cleanse, so it can be exhausting. Pruning, on the other hand (being "cut off" or having things suddenly cut out of your life), can catch you by surprise and even hurt you deeply. Pruning almost always requires a period of healing before future healthy growth can occur.

Both are part of Fall's cycles of letting go and regrowth. As we learn the signs of Fall's approach, we can reduce the chaos that comes along with Fall's lessons of quiet renewal.

Visible Signs

The visual beauty of early Fall can have quite an impact on our senses. I used to live in Southern California. We don't see signs of seasonal changes as dramatically as we do here in North Carolina; however, regardless of one's awareness of the season, tremendous daily activity will be happening both above and below ground during Fall.

As fall approaches, try and notice a subtle shift in reflection of the sunrise through a kitchen window. Colors are more vibrant—the morning's dew, more violet with amber hues not far behind. A rainbow runs the veins of changing leaves. Cool winds stir once securely seated leaves along a branch's limb, sending some spiraling through the air like seasonal public announcements of change. Fall colors beg for us to look upon them, notice them, appreciate their beauty before chaotic winds carry them away.

Fall intends to restore branches to a naked, vulnerable state for the longevity of the fruit-bearing cycle. Yet, Fall is also celebrating the previous summer season of abundant beauty with its cool, stirring winds that beckon us to appreciate the bounty one last time. From a lushly decorated, fruit-producing tree's perspective (if they had one), I surmise Fall could feel sort of like approaching quiet chaos, moving in only to steal all the lush goodness the tree has worked so hard to produce.

Fall winds can be gentle or relentless reminders to stop fighting to hang on and teach us to let go. Of course, there is an inward and outward struggle for most humans to let go gracefully, but the willingness to make an effort is all part of the season's intentional design.

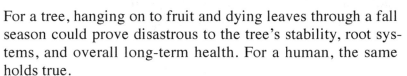

Fall reveals how essential letting go of temporary beauty and comfort is to the overall process of continued growth.

For a tree, hanging on to fruit and dying leaves through a fall season could prove disastrous to the tree's stability, root systems, and overall long-term health. For a human, the same holds true.

Our lives can often feel more chaotic when we are clinging to a hyper-focused view of the temporary things we think create beauty and lush comforts. Fighting the long-term internal and "eternal" strengthening of the spirit that can occur when we are vulnerable only creates more chaos in the seasons ahead. Our temporary body isn't intended to inherit the beauty that belongs to the Spirit. Think of Fall chaos as being less about loss and more about letting go, and you'll begin to receive. We have to learn to let go to redevelop and, in many cases, rediscover a beauty deep within. That is the first step to experiencing peace through what has the potential to become a chaotic Fall process.

 Our growth process starts by letting go.

Fall metaphorically reminds us to let go of the external stuff and focus inward on our spiritual roots. Cleansed, even naked before God, is where we receive immeasurably more beauty, peace, comfort, and strength than we can ever create in our own understanding. Detaching from the things of this world can be wildly chaotic for women at the height of their beauty. The world tends to reward beauty and condemn its loss as if "loss of beauty" is somehow unnatural and irreplaceable. It's Not! The reflection in your bathroom mirror may stir a quiet chaos within you with each (gray hair, laugh line, fill in the blank). Yet, if you understand the season, you can begin to realize that the cool wind you're feeling simply signals a celebration of change that connects to peace rather than chaos. Wait for it.

I've worked with many women dealing with inner and outer beauty image chaos throughout my years in the beauty industry and ministry service. The connecting point to peace for them was experiencing the freedom of letting go rather than viewing their beauty as being lost.

Fall marks for us (men and women) an annual time of surrender, maturity, deeper-rooted beauty, and Christ-centered faith. I'm not suggesting letting go is always comfortable. It rarely is, but it can be a peace-filled process.

Let's try an experiment right now. Look out the window and find a tree with some leaves on it. It does not matter what actual season you are in at the moment; you can always find a tree with leaves somewhere. Now think of each leaf on that tree as representing something you've spent time and energy building up, accumulating, or acquiring throughout your life thus far, things that have brought you comfort or admiration from others. Go for it. It can take a while to make your list, so take the time now to re-educate yourself on where you've spent your youth-filled energy and what you may be continuing to pour your energy into.

Once your list is complete, go back and circle the leaves (accomplishments) that are most significant.

Now, picture cool winds and colorful sunsets like a Fall reflection off of those beautiful leaves. The most beautiful leaves are probably the most temporary ones. Yet, they are, in all likelihood, the exclamation points of the beauty you have placed on your life? Am I right? Jobs change, kids grow, businesses merge, trophies tarnish, people shift.

When Fall hits and starts stirring that stuff around, it's testing with winds what needs to stay and that which needs to go so you can re-focus your energy on your roots, which I will explain in a moment.

I would guess that the thought of the loss of any of the most colorful leaves you've named strikes fear or stirs a quiet sort of chaos within you right now. But, fall is here to remind you that loss is an integral part of anything good and beautiful that is yet to come.

ANYTHING that interferes with the process of letting go or a deeper root system will ultimately hold back a tree from replenishing its foliage or bearing continued fruit in the seasons ahead. Why? Nature is change. Fall is preparing you for an even more vibrant season to come.

With wisdom, sit with the peace of letting go for a moment. Let the hope of peace sink in. It's a choice to be at peace with the chaos of letting go. But, on the other hand, if you want to know how Fall chaos becomes the villain of your life's story, remain stuck in a tug of war with temporal things that God is trying to replenish. The energy lost in that kind of battle will most certainly lead to a disheartened-discontentment with God and others. Including yourself!

Fall teaches us to be comfortable with the stirrings that lead to letting go and ultimately restoration and renewal. God knows us intimately, and you are being seen clearly by a loving God as you let go of the things that have been covering you up. But the real beauty of Fall lingers deep beneath the soil, long after the leaves have dropped. The chaos of quietness and quieting of the chaos meet up in the root system of our life. And I promise I'm going to get to the root system.

But I just want to check in with you here and be completely honest about how hard it was and still can be for me to let go.

A Deep Personal Cleansing

During one particularly complicated and chaotic Fall cycle, I heard God's voice speaking to me very clearly through Scripture. He was calming that season's chaos by reminding me I would always be enough and have enough. I had been feeling empty, exposed, and broken as a byproduct of a difficult emotional betrayal. God was offering me the opportunity to let go of my grasp on the one thing that represented love to me. In its place, he showed me how to remain calm before the force of His winds and find a deeper-rooted, emotional maturity with the Creator of love itself, Christ.

The more I fought to let go of the idea of a temporal love I desperately wanted to hang on to, the more I was setting myself up for a good Fall pruning. However, through consistent Scripture reading, I was encouraged to securely fasten my roots deep in Him no matter how chaotic my loss was feeling (I share more about this season in "Story Time").

A wisdom-filled girlfriend reminded me to stop trying to hang on to what my Fall season was trying to blow down. She also reminded me that a Fall cleansing cycle is not about making me worthy of God's love (his love is a guarantee regardless of how we make it through each season), but the cleansing helps free us from the toxins that bind us to chaos! So I decided to let go and re-focus my energy on my roots and relationship with Christ. He promised that I would be rested, renewed, and restored by the season's end! And I was.

Cleansing for Root Health.

Cleansing prepares us to withstand the tremendous amount of abundance God has in store for us just a few seasons ahead. You might not see worldly fruits (or leaves) as temporary as God does, but fruits and leaves that are being blown down during a fall cleansing cycle are decaying anyway. No matter how precious or how beautiful these fruits seem to the world, these are the things that will soon be keeping your *energy* away from your roots. As the season intentionally diverts all energy back towards your roots in Christ, you begin to learn to quiet the striving for the things in the world.

What "leaves or fruit" are you hanging on to instead of hanging on to Him? Is it working, positioning, performing, earning, longings? (How does this apply to you? Perhaps journal your thoughts and feelings here.) If you take the time to ask Him, he will show you what is keeping your energy away from deepening your roots, that you might grow deeper in Christ's love.

Take this time of chaos and let God bring you into this time of naked truth with him. It is an essential but often overlooked opportunity for stability and security. Once your distractions and limitations are removed, energy from every limb and branch in your life is more easily concentrated into your maturity process.

Meeting Him in naked truth about the health of your life with Him or others is an opportunity for a very intimate time of inspection and blessing by Him. But, on the other hand, fighting an inevitable season of loss can feel like a chaotic wind storm blowing in over your life. Picture leaves swept up in every direction, and good fruits being blown to the ground, half-broken limbs tossed every which way. Messy.

God desires to see us clearly, but, more importantly, he wants you to know yourself honestly. Loss may be a way He points out your diseased branches, dying fruits, and the moldy leaves that will keep you from abundance in the seasons ahead. His plans are always good. To fight him puts our well-being at stake, and it only makes it harder on us in the long run.

I've had to get over a lot of insecurity. To do that, I've had to go deep into the soil of Christ intentionally. By absorbing His Word into my life, I was able to claim His freedoms and peace. Connecting myself to Him with deeper roots is what brings peace in the windstorms of my life. With each season, my relationship deepens, and faith grows larger fruits. Trusting Christ in his Word and letting go of outcomes has given me incredible self-esteem. I let Him see me at my worst, and somehow He makes me feel good about seeing the real me. How often do we let that happen in our lives, intentionally?

Deep roots give me the security to stand firm under the chaotic opinion of others. With stable spiritual roots, you can more easily identify and let go of vanity, material and superficial attachments, chaotic relationships, pridefulness, people-pleasing, insecurity, and fear in general. My Fall experiences (in hindsight) have all equipped me with the confidence to encourage you right now. I can assure you that God will bring you beauty and abundant fruit in the seasons to come. Even if onlookers can only see chaos, you'll be able to appreciate the beauty of the season because everything good is happening beneath the surface, on the inside, in your roots.

> **Confidence in Christ's Word is what brings your inward beauty of hope outward and the outward beauty of hope confidently inward.**

A Good Pruning

Once you quietly settle into Fall's rhythm of letting go, you're going to find yourself less dense (excuse the pun), and the real you is less hidden. But a word about the pain and promise of pruning; Since we just don't know what we don't know until we know it, we have to allow room in our lives for the pain of Godly pruning to reveal His wisdom within us. Within His intentional pruning of our worldly strongholds, He is creating space in us for His wisdom to rise through our root system, thus creating vibrant life fruits that we could have never brought forth in our own strength and limited understanding.

Let me further clarify that Pruning is a "part" of cleansing, but they are not the same. They will feel very different, but they are both parts of the same cleaning cycle.

First, Fall allows for the gradual and gentle blowing away of foliage. Then, once we have learned to be secure and patient about letting go, Fall's cycle offers us another opportunity to grow with stabilized roots. That means roots in relationship with Christ. Then and only then are we offered an intimate and possible pruning session by God Himself. After all, He is the ultimate creator and caretaker of our root system and our forever fruits in Christ from that point forever forward.

Absolute chaos can happen during a Fall cycle when we do not acknowledge that "cutting back" or "cutting away" is part of the process of achieving more growth. Only God can see the intricate parts of our life, and He is so very purposeful in His pruning when necessary. But the cutting away of anything we are attached to, that has become a part of us… well, it's just going to sting. This purposeful pruning is going to require a faith-filled time to heal the wounds properly. God is only removing things that will ultimately cause us to suffer in the long run during this process — but only if you let Him. He will not allow hurt to go unused, but you have to trust Him through it and with it. By allowing God to prune us and shape us, we experience God's offering of active love.

Yes! A purposeful pruning is a healing act of love built right into a cycle of a winter resting, spring building, and ultimately summer fruiting again! When we stop fighting the process by which we are being strengthened and loved, there is a quieting of the pain, and healing begins. That's when the chaos stops feeling so chaotic.

Intentional Wounds

To address pain in a new light, let's visit the notion of creating a "wound" intentionally. As a gardener, I know an excellent late Spring or early Fall pruning is mainly about the purposeful cutting away of chaos-making-disease-inviting-burdens from my trees. It is done for the benefit of my trees' abundant future. When I see one of my trees producing diseased fruit, I know this tree will continue to do so until I intervene, or it runs out of energy and dies. So I prune the things away from my tree that my tree can't or won't eliminate on its own. Since I (as the gardener and caretaker of my tree) can identify what is no longer healthy for the longevity of the fruit-bearing ability of the tree, I very intentionally go about the process of pruning, cutting, and removing anything that I believe will get in the way of my tree's good health.

I may even remove one or two perfectly healthy branches. Yes, sometimes I'll cut off even a few healthy limbs, not to injure the tree, but to help shape the tree's future. By removing a few specific healthy branches, I can force growth onto another area of the tree that may not have produced growth otherwise. My wounding is specific and designed with the tree's maturity and health in mind.

Intentional Healing

Healing is a crucial part of the pruning process. I take my time with the pruning of my trees. I'm selective and careful about the limbs I take and the time of year I am taking them. I am very intentional about the required healing process I am expecting to put my trees through. In other words, I'm very aware of the health of my tree's root system and its ability to produce the energy necessary to recover from the pruning and cleansing experience.

Now, let's say a neighbor jumped my fence, picked up some pruning shears, and started hacking away at my trees with no rhyme or reason to it. There is a huge potential for damage and disease to occur in my orchard through those reckless cuttings. I would have to assist my tree's healing process from that assault in a completely different way than from my intentional pruning process. If my tree's root system is deep and stable, it's plausible the assaulted tree would be capable of recovering on its own. But if my tree's root system is shallow, or the tree was overburdened with dense diseased foliage, it is quite possible the tree would go into a state of shock from such an attack.

Some attacks are brutal to recover from-not impossible but certainly chaotic. Healing and recovering from an assault we were never intentioned to endure is a process that must be nurtured season after season.

There are some things God just never intended for us to experience. Some injuries can be healed with the help of a new perspective of the pain. Some injuries we experience will require more attention and healing reconciliation before we can expect to see growth return to those wounded areas of our lives. With any amount of faith in Christ, we can begin the recovery process from virtually anything this world throws at us or takes from us.

If God is doing the purposeful pruning in your life, pruning will be good no matter how chaotic the experience is. If God is not doing the pruning, then pain is a reality, and the healing of forgiveness may be your best and only option if you want to find peace or quietness with that kind of chaos. Just remember, with deeper roots in Christ, you can withstand anything with forgiveness because God stands there with you-maybe even between you and the chaos.

Fall and Forgiveness

> **To forgive a wrong done to you is to reconcile it.**

That word reconciliation has "roots" (again with the puns) in the Greek word allasso (ajllavssw). Commonly meaning "change." Christ is the change-master. There must be a change in relationship, from brokenness to fellowship, for the healing to occur. When you sink your roots deeper into Christ's kind of change for your life, you'll find reconciliation with others the most peaceful parts of your process of growth, even when it looks or feels like chaos.

> **If you hold God responsible, however, for the assaults this world has placed upon you, you're going to have a challenging time healing those wounds until you've reconciled your relationship with God first.**

Think about that for a moment.

I interviewed many women who blamed God for pruning wounds allowed by God but made by humanity. Now, you may be asking why a loving God would allow hurts to occur in the first place. The simple answer is "free will."

But the more complicated, faith-filled answer is; we actually may not fully understand all the why's this side of Heaven. But I can tell you this: Women able to discern the difference between the pain of God's purposeful pruning and the reckless pruning of mankind (who had reconciled the idea that God didn't cause their pain, people did), and then trusted God could repurpose their pain for good if they gave it to Him in faith, they were the women who purposefully moved forward in their life, with peace.

In addition to reconciled suffering, they also discovered the fruit (or wisdom) of the experiences. Women who had let go of their past bitterness and pain were soon sharing and aiding in healing others who had experienced similar injuries as theirs.

God will never waste your hurts, heartaches, hardships or humility!

Fall's cleansing, pruning, and healing cycles can prepare and establish confidence within us for the purposeful [1]mission God has already called our life to in Christ. Roots of change in Christ stabilize us with His mercy and grace. It allows us to become better versions of ourselves season after season. [2]New Creations!

Past Failures

The kindest and most healing thing I've ever done for myself is to reconcile my past mistakes with God. I've often found the hardest person to forgive is quite literally myself. And I've been

---

[1] . Acts 20:24 NCV *"The most important thing is that I complete my mission, the work that the Lord Jesus gave me-to tell people the Good News about God's grace"*

[2] . 2 Cor 5:17 NIV *"Therefore, if anyone is in Christ, he is a new creation; the old has gone, the new has come!"*

able to allow God's plan to quiet that chaos as well. In return, I learn something useful from each experience.

We are not our failures; we are so much more than those moments.

Forgiveness, mercy, and grace reconcile the deepest, most painful errors you've ever made or can imagine. Grace simply heals them then and there. The redemptive power of forgiveness quiets chaos. We learn to trust God through the processes of forgiving and being forgiven. Once we've figured out how to relax and truly trust God with our pains and our praise, we can then assist others in the process of how to do the same.

I know. It's easier said than done. Seriously, I know how difficult it is to "forgive." It's one thing to say the words of forgiveness; it quite literally requires something intentional to practice and apply. All God asks is that we try, then learn to lean on His power rather than our own to accomplish it.

I am encouraged to grow in quiet confidence by returning to a Fall reconciliation process every fourth season, not by chance but by grace-filled design.

Encouragement time!

If you're not inspired by the concept of reconciling, pruning, or a naked submitting before God, I get it. I understand how difficult trying to "be" encouraging to others is when you still try to understand the season and process yourself. (If you Work in ministry—you know what I am talking about).

Just know that you'll be, and—you—are okay, just as you are. The world may require us to get it all together just to be seen or heard, but we don't have to be all cleaned up to come before God. Ever! We can come as dirty and messy, broken, diseased, or overburdened as we are. Just come true and authentic before Him as you are right now. You're not able to hide your chaos and messiness from Him anyway, so why put even an ounce of energy into trying to do that!

> **Instead, save your energy for sending your roots deeper into the mercy and grace part of this experience with Him.**

Confused, hurt, angry, mad, entitled, justified … pick a word. It's okay. You are okay. Just be honest with yourself and with God. God knows who you are and what He is doing with you. He wants YOU to know who you are, so be honest with yourself even if it hurts. God hurts when you hurt, or others hurt you. He, too, cries when you cry, even as He prunes and removes branches from your life. God understands loss. He understands suffering. He understands you may struggle with faith, faith in Him, faith in the process, faith in good coming out of the chaos, or even faith that any of this even really matters at all. He understands all of it. He gets it because Christ lived it.

In your pain and chaos, God is giving you the opportunity to be seen, truly seen, and to be set free from the delusion of you trying to keep it all together in your own strength. Although you may not completely understand His process, just learn to give Him more of your hurts, pains, frustrations, and disappointments at every new opportunity, and He will soon quiet the chaos of it all. I know that sounds like a lot, but it is less complicated than it sounds.

If you are unsure where to start, just flip to the "Invitation" in the back of this book and start there. Simply talk to God. Tell him how you're feeling and what you're thinking. There is a freeing that comes with that part of the process itself. It quiets your chaos and redirects your energy. Don't judge how messy it is. God already knows you are having a hard time during this process, but He wants YOU to know YOU are capable of finding His quieting in this chaos, but it has to be in His strength rather than your own. That may very well even be the reason He is allowing the chaos in the first place: to allow you to discover Him fully by choice.

By [3]trusting the process until the cleansing and pruning are complete and the season has transitioned, you will have discovered an incredible peace to process future moments of chaos as well as abundance. Plus, you will find growing gratitude for things you never even realized were possible until you let go of them.

There is a season of real Winter rest just ahead. You're almost there. Hang on.

Carry A Burden

Part of the healing and maturity process may often include sacrifice, but not in the way you might be thinking. Sacrifice is not just the giving up of something you want to hang on to; it could mean carrying the weight of something you would rather discard.

Forcing a cleansing or pruning upon oneself or another out of fear, convenience, vanity, greed, impatience, arrogance,

---

[3] . *Mark 10:29-30 (TBL)* Jesus replied *"Let me assure you that no one has ever given up anything...for love of me and to tell others the Good News, who won't be given back, a hundred times over... All these will be his here on earth, and in the world to come he shall have eternal life."*

pridefulness or envy, will always land us in chaos. God has to prepare our hearts first, and only He can set the proper timing for release. Preparing our hearts could mean we need to acquire new skills over several seasons so our roots and structure can support and carry the weight of what He is asking us to carry.

A heavy fruitless limb may seem a logical choice to prune, so it won't always make logical sense if you are called to carry it. But wisdom will lead you. Knowledge without wisdom can lead to pride, vanity, and more chaos. God may intend (as He often does in nature) for heavy but empty limbs to linger. They may not be especially beautiful to look at; they might require extra energy to support, especially during storms, but removing them for the sake of personal satisfaction is harmful to what's happening in the spiritual root system of your life.

Christ may desire to see fruit in abundance from that limb one day, and for that limb to bear fruit, He may be entrusting you to provide the unsightly, heavy, naked limb with proper care through a tough chaotic, or quiet season.

Through a season of sacrificial obedience and perseverance, we learn to resist the temptations of convenience and stand firm in the face of fear. We can learn to withstand the Heavenly weight of sacrifice for the benefit of ourselves or others. Replacing a heavy weight with a Heavenly weight requires our hope to be in Him alone and not in our own comfort or discomfort. Remember, it's just a season. It will pass in a very short time compared to eternity. Any chaotic sacrifice will require deep roots in Christ to experience peace through the chaos. Wisdom will help you discern the right-next-thing to do when faced with decisions during this type of season.

Okay, I'm going to be brave. I am going to share some of my own pruning mistakes with you. I made a few of them during some chaotic cycles in my life. Why am I sharing my messiness with you? Because I truly believe God will never waste our chaos, and when we are brave enough to share our failure, others may realize they are not alone in their own chaotic seasons too.

My Own Unnecessary Wounding

I can recall a season in my life when fear and pain were super intense for me. My reflex response was to throw myself into an unnatural pruning cycle to remove whatever it was that felt like a threat to me. But during this one particular season of chaos, I began cutting away ideas, hopes, dreams, projects, even people from my life that God never asked me to remove. In hindsight, He was calling me to love a big empty and extremely heavy branch in my life more fully. But I was hurting, and the heaviness of the season hurt me, so I hacked away at the things that felt heavy to me.

See, I had some real wounds from childhood that had never healed properly and had slowed my roots from absorbing the spiritual nutrients necessary to discern the difference between carrying a burden in faith and submitting to shaping by the hand of God. What I am trying to say is that I was selfish and spiritually immature. Though I presented myself to the world as a warrior, I did so only to hide that I alternated between chaos cycles of fear and pride. I was cutting things out of my life to ease my fleshy suffering but presented as a strong, capable woman who wouldn't take shizzel from anyone. I didn't know that at the time, or I would have stopped striving then and there, but I didn't, so I couldn't.

Rather than listening for God's voice in the season, I only paid attention to my feelings and the noise of the chaos. Eventually, I became desperate, and I felt alone and out of energy most of the time, yet I continued whacking away at things trying to lighten my own burdens. All the life force God had intended to use, to teach me to persevere through injury from others, was being diverted to heal the unnecessary wounds I was giving to myself. My self-pruning was wounding God had never intended for me to suffer through.

Eventually, my self-pruning created chaotic-uncontrolled-rolled-up-in-a-ball-on-the-bathroom-floor, knees-to-my-chest, Bible-thrown-across the-room, why-does-everyone-abandon-me, -I-can't-take-it-any-more, kind of crying. I mean wet—soggy—buckets—full!

Now, any good gardener will tell you not to prune limbs when it's wet outside. That kind of pruning creates wounds that attract and invites disease, parasites, and improper healing to arise. And I was soggy! The more I cut out of my life, the deeper I fell into chaotic quietness and self-isolation. I pushed people away that were there to help me because my pride wouldn't let anyone else pick up the pieces, clean up my mess, or help me heal. I didn't trust anyone but myself.

But I was clearly my own worst enemy.

My self-tormenting went on for several seasons. On the outside, I managed to clean myself up and present like I had it all together, but my wounds went straight to my heart and created wounds upon wounds. Resentment and spiritual disease traveled right on in through those poorly healed areas never meant to be cut off in the first place. But because God is a compassionate gardener, He kept sending His workers out to look after my wounds. He tended to me and waited upon me, Fall after Fall cycle, sending healer after healer. He was allowing me time to heal and learn to trust He would never give up on me. Not only did that begin to reassure me I could trust Him with my pain, but it reassured me I could place my faith in Him rather than myself during those chaotic painful cycles, and they were really painful.

Slowly I became healthier, and my wounds began to heal, and as they did, I became clearer about the discomforts that were meant for my good to endure. As my chaos began to quiet in Him, the quietness was less chaotic, and I began to notice I was becoming fruitful in the areas I had once abandoned. I think the most difficult season of healing is actually where my heart for ministry service grew.

Today, I can honestly say that my commitment to listening and waiting upon the Lord is more important than my comfort. By letting God direct my steps, I learned to let go of what I thought my life "should" look like and began to live it out as only God showed me it could look like.

When I experienced the true redemptive power and reconciliation of Christ-like love, my chaos stopped being so chaotic. Who knew! God has always loved me like that, but it was through proper pruning, cleansing, and healing, that I am now much more capable of loving others as Christ loves me.

> **With roots in Christ, chaos stops feeling so chaotic, pruning stops feeling so painful, cleansing starts feeling more freeing, and Christ-like burdens start feeling much lighter.**

I promise.

Living for Christ In a PC World

The more PC our world is becoming, the more it's going to feel like our God-given freedoms are being pruned from us. People are exercising their right to cut away things from our life that God intended for His glory. It's a painful part of improper pruning by the hand of humanity.

The loss of freedom for freedom's sake is like a disease that rapidly spreads from tree to tree, generation after generation, until eventually, the entire orchid produces a different kind of inedible fruit altogether.

You can read about this happening throughout the Old Testament. Time after time, humanity is reminding itself through history about the need for a savior, all the while bad stuff is happening to good people. God gives humanity a choice to live life His way or our own, but everyone is susceptible to the poor choice consequences of others.

Humanity is free from coercion on God's part to choose Christ. And even if we do choose Christ, we can still make poor free-will choices born of immaturity. I like to compare that to a lack of a deep root system in Him. But God refuses to take back humanity's freedom to choose. No matter how diseased an orchard becomes, God is calling us, one by one, to Himself in Christ. It is by His hand He will prune us to drive our roots deeper in Him, but He will not burn down the entire orchard until the day that humanity recognizes how much it needs to be saved from itself. The only way to survive the chaos of human mistakes that cause injury is to have deep roots in Christ.

As a Jesus girl, I believe with all of my heart that only Jesus saves. Humanity's pruning of it cannot silence his Truth Sending our roots deeper into Christ is the only thing that will bring peace when you are being attacked by humanity's good or bad pruning intentions. I'm also a firm believer that only those with deep roots in Christ will withstand that final Fall cleansing and healing cycle when it comes upon us.

But until then, we must simply focus on our roots and let God take care of our fruits. Then, we can continue to thrive in a world that is becoming increasingly full of disease-packing-modified-fruit-seed-rotting-hatchet-swinging-human-so-called "saviors."

How do we thrive as the world is trying to cut us down? By trusting that God has planted us where He wants us to grow those roots. We will thrive in the orchard He has called us to, and our abundance will come in His timing, not ours. Don't worry about your fruit or your foliage. In humanity's final Fall cleansing cycle, it won't much matter what the fruit of survival, success, thriving, or persevering looks like. Still, an eternal peace-filled everlasting life with God is your reward for withstanding the cycle. Time itself is in short supply here on earth, but there is an endless offering of time in Christ. What may feel like chaos today gives life meaning tomorrow and for eternity.

Your life can be used for good rather than allowing the chaos to use you. Just don't give up and don't judge what God is doing. You will experience purpose in your chaos. He is expressing Himself through you if you let Him. It is all part of a cleansing cycle toward growth. God is not cutting joy out of your life; He is preparing you for an abundance of it—in Him—for eternity!

Hang on. The Story Isn't Over.

Story Time

Just as one's experience can be profound in the living, sharing that story can be an important part of life to the next generation. God's truth plays out through real-life experiences. Not just the idea of who He is, but the actual life expression of faith in Him that is exposed when someone is brave enough to share their story of life with Him, with others.

As I sit here typing, trying to decide which story would be the most fruitful for this first chapter, (I mean, now that I've shared some of my ugly chaos already, I may as well keep going, right?), I glance over at my coffee cup, which reads, "You are not perky. You are obnoxious." The other side reads, "Your enthusiasm is scaring everyone." This cup is a gift I purchased for myself while on a girl's trip recently. I purchased it because, while I like to draw out Story from others and share mine, wisdom has taught me that[4] what I say, the way I say it, and when I share it all have an impact (negative or positive) on the fruitfulness of the sharing.

Basically, timing is everything.

On more than one occasion, I've tried to positively impact a life with storytelling, and the timing, the words, or the situation was not right. The story was not well received, and rather than providing joy; chaos was the reward for the effort. My little coffee cup reminds me to check my perkiness and my enthusiasm for Christ before the joyful sharing of it.

So I settled on the following story because I want you to hear how silly I am when chatting with God over something as simple as joy. This season was a quiet but deeply chaotic season for me. The joy stealing issue I was wrestling with at the time

---

[4] . *Colossians 4:6 NIV Let your conversation be always full of grace, seasoned with salt, so that you may know how to answer everyone.*

was an incredibly sensitive subject, and my goal is to be honest but respectful to not place blame on anyone or anything other than my own spiritual immaturity (or maturity, depending on how you view it), at the time.

For this book, several people I interviewed shared how difficult it was for them to just talk to God about how they felt or what they were thinking. So I hope that by giving you a glimpse into just one of the ways I come quietly but chaotically before the Savior of my soul, in silly daily conversation, you might have a good laugh at me while permitting yourself to be just a little silly, but honest with God yourself.

Enjoy.

Quiet Chaos

One day I was driving my usual morning commute to work. It had been a particularly long month of grinding away on numbers to meet goals set by ambitious leaders. I was unusually singing out loud to some spunky tune on the radio on that drive. But not today. No reaching-for-notes-I-can't-sing-but-as-long-as-the-windows-are-up-I-didn't-care kind of moment's that morning.

Nope. I was just silent.

It was an awkward silence with myself. I let a series of God's pruning questions interrogate my thought process about Joy that day.

Where is my joy today? Have I lost it? How is that even possible? Joy is supposed to be happening on the inside, deep down in my soul, regardless of my circumstances. How can I lose that!? Maybe I'm just not happy? God, am I not happy? Ohhh, maybe you're not happy with me? Is that it? No, that's silly. How can you be unhappy with me? Wait, why are we talking about happiness anyway? We were talking about joy. Happiness is something I show and experience on the outside and depends on what is happening "to" me, not "in" me.

Hmmmm... I pondered, still sitting quietly in my chaos for a moment more. My mind began searching my memory for a time in scripture when Jesus wasn't happy and then landed on the example of when Jesus was sad. It happened when Jesus's friend [5]Lazarus died. Well, Jesus was "moved." But I guess that could be sad? He certainly felt sad about the way the people of Israel [6]treated Him. So, maybe it was okay then to just feel sad for a day?

Then I thought maybe I just don't know what I'm feeling?

Hey God, what am I feeling? I haven't lost anyone today, and I'm not hanging on a cross. Hmmm? But of course, it's okay to feel sad. But am I sad? No, I don't think I'm sad. So what do I have to be sad about? I'm just...

I began taking a personal inventory over the past week's activities. I was excited about achieving team goals, but something was shifting in our team dynamics. I couldn't articulate it, but I was noticing a shift in stress levels increasing in the leaders I served with. Leaders were making it clear if goals were not achieved, there would be a consequence. For those with job title security, that meant lateral movement. For those without

---

[5] *. John 11:33 When Jesus saw her weeping, and the Jews who had come along with her also weeping, he was deeply moved in spirit and troubled.*

[6] *. Isaiah 53:3 He was despised and rejected by mankind, a man of suffering, and familiar with pain. Like one from whom people hide their faces, he was despised, and we held him in low esteem.*

job title security, it meant being replaced by a male with job title security.

Side note here, I thought about taking that last line out of my story. I struggled with it, but I purposefully left that part in because it was the truth of what I was struggling with at the time. I would never want to shed a negative light on the church or its leaders. I am only sharing this intimate detail of my struggle because it was a difficult issue I needed mentoring for during the season of chaos I am sharing with you. I'm not sure my story would make as much sense without that little detail. See, I was a woman working in ministry long and hard hours with a team of pioneers charged with many firsts for what is now a global platform. I was giving my all to what I felt God had called me to do with my time, talents, treasures, and gifts. But several years and tears in, I began struggling with the issue of not having a voice in things I was passionate about simply because I was a woman. I understand scripture is clear on roles and responsibilities in the church, but at the time, there were very few ways a mostly male pastoral staff could mentor a woman working in my position. Pastors had men's lunches, training, and retreats together. Weekends away nourished pastors' wives together. Even the women working in children's ministry or child care had their own gatherings. But for a woman working in the labor of a pastoral role- there was just no place to be refilled and mentored through the process. So I struggled. I even enrolled in seminary studies in hopes of finding answers to the issues I was deeply moved by, and I finally got them.

I've since put those issue and many others to rest as God has given me a voice in the garden He has called me to grow.

So let's return to my tale of pray-talking with God and leave the rest at His feet.

So, where was I? Oh yes, the silence in my car meeting up with the chaotic Fall winds in my mind. For me, driving radio silent usually meant I was working out whatever question was on my mind while expecting God to meet me in them and calm the storms. Normally He would. But not so on this particular morning. The silent and chaotic questioning just kept getting more intense with each passing moment. I continued on with my self-interrogation, not willing to accept the silence.

Okay, God. What is up? Jesus you are the perfect example of joy that comes from hanging out with God. [7]You have always been with Him and have brought His [8]Spirit in you here on earth, so I have access to that kind of Joy IN me too, right!? So why am I not feeling it this morning? And why are you not answering me? Or are you answering me with your silence? Uhhhh, this silence is frustrating! Jesus, what did you do when you were frustrated? I guess you [9]prayed... a lot. Hmmm, should I be praying for more joy then? Is joy something I can even pray for? [10]I should be joyful. Why am I not joyful? Should I be praying for more happiness or faith instead of joy? Yes, praying for more happiness. That's a good idea. Does praying for that stuff even work though? No, I don't want just happiness, I want joy. I want joy! I like joy. I like the way joy feels inside me and makes me feel about the world around me. So Joy then. But joy isn't actually a feeling though, is it? Nope. Joy is a choice.

Sigh...

---

[7] . John 1:1-2, NIV *In the beginning was the Word, and the Word was with God, and the Word was God. He was with God in the beginning.*

[8] . John 1:14 NIV *The Word became flesh and made his dwelling among us. We have seen his glory, the glory of the one and only Son, who came from the Father, full of grace and truth.*

[9] . Luke 5:16 NIV *But Jesus often withdrew to lonely places and prayed.*

[10] . Psalm 16:11 NIV *You make known to me the path of life; you will fill me with joy in your presence, with eternal pleasures at your right hand.*

Well, when I have joy, I'm nicer to the people around me. I'm less critical and much funnier too. I can't choose to be funny or less critical, can I? No. Well... maybe? Okay, yes! So praying for joy is a good thing then, right!? If joy makes me a better me, don't you want me to have more of it? So, I might as well pray for more joy then..."

There was no external noise in my life louder than my own internal noise as I drove on that morning. What would look to an outsider as silence instead was the chaos of that quietness. That is what pushed the conversation forward in my head. I continued "pray-talking" for what felt like hours.

Okay, I just read somewhere that extraordinary results come from confidence and willingness to choose what matters most in any situation. Okay. But I also have to be willing to give to what matters most, the proper amount of time it demands. Okay, so maybe I'm out of balance this morning. Am I out of balance, God? Or are my priorities mixed up? [11]*Acting on priorities means the right things take precedence when they should, and what's leftover gets done when I can get to it. Okay. Intentional chaos. It's purposeful and useful. So, should I check in to ensure my priorities are in order and my counterbalance in Christ is strong?*

I got out of my head for a moment and noticed it was cloudy and overcast outside. I'm one of those super-sensitive SDD (Seasonal Defective Disorder) people. Yes, it's a real thing. I struggle when the sun does not come out. I'm a born and raised Cali girl now living in North Carolina. Sunshine is like food to me. So, there was that thing happening. In addition, my husband had been out of town for the past two weeks straight. Kevin is my rock, my sounding board, and encourager. When he's gone, I spend way more time in my head than is probably productive. So, there was that too.

---

[11] . "The One Thing" by Gary Keller

Then I began thinking of the other contributing factors that might have led to the kind of quiet chaos of my prayer talk with God that morning.

I love being around people, but I get and give my best self with four or five long-term besties. And guess what, they were all out of town hanging out in some sunny part of the world together, and I had stayed behind to follow through on work commitments. (One of those heavy branches we were talking about that would have been easier to just self-prune off, but I had already learned my lesson on that subject). I felt a little resentful of the so-called "sacrifice" my work required of me that morning. I also recognized that I was becoming mentally and emotionally exhausted of the "grind" that work had become. The systems of work had somehow become my master. Instead of the systems serving me, I had begun serving the systems. My balance/counterbalance needed some reprioritizing.

> **In the quiet moments of my chaos that morning, God was ever so silently pointing me back to the space inside of me where new possibilities were supposed to be growing, but the past was taking up the space where joy in the present was supposed to live!**

It was then that I realized important priorities had been pushed out of place by things I was still holding on to from my past. I immediately turned my car around and headed back home to begin doing something I had been procrastinating for more than a year. I needed to put some closure to things I had built up in the past. It was the only way I would become empowered rather than restricted by them moving forward.

I called work and told them I was taking a personal day. I had piles of binders and papers from work projects and ideas that were delayed, died, or rejected. These binders represented bodies of work I was passionate about in seasons past, but they never got the opportunity to bear fruit; however, holding on to them was not making them fruitful either.

I spent the entire morning playing praise music and tossing away my old agendas. I was finally obedient to the cleansing God called me to a year earlier, yet only just now willing to do. I found my joy that morning by inviting Christ to have complete freedom to redirect the work of my heart and hands and, I was getting a fresh way of thinking from Him.

By lunchtime, I was exhausted. I decided to head over to a local coffee shop just to take a break from myself. The drive remained silent, but there was a difference in the silence now. There was a peacefulness to the quietness. I started to think about the times I had spent on the mission field. It's where I learned a great deal about connecting to people's stories and joy. I met many people with far less favorable living conditions than me, yet joy was alive despite their conditions.

After each trip, I would return home more appreciative of the things I took for granted on the daily like; community, family, a hot bath of water, or simply a drink of water.

That opened up a whole new place for gratitude to pour out of my mind. Right then and there, I ran with that filling up of gratitude. I started to thank God that He had purposefully pruned my husband and my friends from my life for the entire week to have me all to Himself and for my own good. My roots went deeper in Christ that morning, and I was grateful for that. God taught me to "choose my joy," and in so doing, I was reclaiming my happiness with His goodness.

Still, in my chaotic silence, I finally quieted my mind. Only then was I able to hear God's voice and see something besides me. That is when I realized I was entering a season of rest.

> **I had to learn how to move from serving goals to serving Him. Only then could I truly find joy in serving others.**

Comfort, rest, and peace were on the horizon. My Winter season had finally arrived!

~Winter~

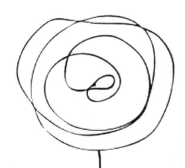

Chaos & Quietness of Winter

"Peace I leave with you, my peace I give you.
I do not give to you as the world gives.
Do not let your hearts be troubled and do not be afraid."

John 14:27 NIV

Rest / Comfort

Winter moves into slow me down, even causes me to rest or start over. What Type A person likes having her roll slowed, even just a little? But God uses Winter to slow this fast-paced girl down for my own good. In Winter's rest, I'm comforted and find I write my best story.

I love Story. Story is an intentional instrument I use to encourage people through shifting seasons in their lives. That is why I'm writing this book. The best parts of every good story I've ever heard or told are the ones with hope-filled triumphs over the chaos that attacks our hearts and steals our peace.

Unquieted, uncontrolled Winter chaos flips everything around. "Dids" turn to "would haves" then to "could haves," and guilty chaos follows that up with "should haves," and on it goes. But with a little understanding of this Winter cycle, we will find Fall has deepened our roots to hold us steady if a chaotic storm of Winter hits.

Past the words of childhood, past the hurts, past the fear, past the frantic pace of life, we can emerge from Winter triumphant and rested. For me, I emerge as an encourager, equipped with enough personal Story of hope-filled experiences about triumphs over the chaos that changes the lives of others.

Hope is the glue that holds everything in proper perspective. My hope-filled chaotic seasons even got me wondering if chaos was connected somehow to the process of maturing our hope into faith? The quieting of chaos all comes down to what we place our hope in. Hope is the essential tool we have to have to successfully navigate the chaos and even make peace with it.

With a hope-infused perspective and a little courage, chaos starts looking more like the thunder clouds that ultimately bring in the rainbows rather than the lightning behind those clouds that usher in a storm.

I'm praying you are beginning to find a fresh new view of chaos as we enter Winter together. There is so much goodness a season of Winter's rest can bring.

Yes, rest is where we are heading now.

Rest is, after all, part of the natural cycle of things. All that Fall cleansing, pruning, and healing require some downtime to recover from, so Winter is the perfect place to be. [12]Winter is a season that calls for a full body restorative stilling. It's more than a simple sleeping; it's a slowing and silencing that brings comfort, quietness, and peace. It's not just a pause of the work of our hands; it's a trusting rest in Him that brings completeness to surrender and purpose.

> **Winter is where we learn to trust that He will protect us as we rest in Him while He carries us the distance we would have lamented having to walk on our own.**

But if you are here with me in Winter yet doubtful, even feeling like the storm of the century has moved chaos in over your rest, I have a spin on that chaos that just might bring you to peace.

Follow me through these Winter metaphors, and feel free to bring your doubts with you. Being doubtful is like being restless; it's a normal process of adapting to a chaotic season. Storms can cause fear. Fear can cause doubt. Doubt can cause movement. God can still them all. So bring your restlessness before the Creator of the seasons Himself.

Even if you doubt Christ, you'll begin to appreciate what Winter is trying to teach. [13]God assures us that in quietness with Him, He has gone ahead of us to do for us what we cannot do for ourselves. It starts with the opportunity to submit our hearts to Him and lose track of time within His arms, covered by a blanket of his coolness— for an entire season.

As He is holding us, we fall more in love with Jesus. He will show us how. Now, I'm not talking about the passionate

---

[12] . *Psalms 91:1 (NIV) Whoever dwells in the shelter of the Most High will rest in the shadow of the Almighty.*

[13] . *Matthew 6:6 "But when you pray, go into your room and shut the door and pray to your Father who is in secret. And your Father who sees in secret will reward you."*

presumptions we bring about love as a man or a woman. I'm talking about a love that is grace-filled in ways it takes acceptance to understand. To accept God's love requires a submission of the heart that is hidden from human eyes, but God knows when it is there. God cares about how you feel and about what you do and the stillness of Winter is like a great revealer of the intentions of your heart.

> **God is much more concerned with your intentions than your activities during this season.**

The more you trust Him the more you love Him. The more you love Him [14]the more you want to follow His will for your life. Sometimes standing still to be loved requires everything within you to be calmed first for your mind and heart to receive that love. But beware. There is another side to a stillness that is dark and dangerous and more chaotic than any kind of doubt.

It's called indifference.

I've never personally experienced the chaos of indifference in my own life. I don't say that pridefully but almost embarrassingly. I'm too passionately opinionated to be indifferent. But I have witnessed the quiet chaos indifference has brought into the lives of others. Indifference might mimic doubt, but indifference doesn't seek. At least doubt keeps you moving to seek and see God's face in the restless chaos of your Winters. Indifference, however, is paralyzing. The immobility of indifference has you giving up hope altogether. That is not peaceful rest. It is death.

Let's look at something as innocent as making Winter snow angels. If you intentionally go outside to make a snow angel, not a big deal. You'll probably put on some warm winter clothing,

---

[14] . *John 14:15 – If you love Me, you will keep my commandments.*

invite a friend to join in the fun, and head back inside when you get too cold from the Winter's snow. But in a season of indifference, it could be in the dead middle of a Winter storm when you wander outside. Naked without God's protection, unsupervised and indifferent, you play in the snow until exhaustion, then just lay there, by yourself, in the cold of Winter, and freeze to death— by choice—in quiet indifference and silence.

Let's seek out some better options together as we continue on with our metaphors surrounding a Winter's rest under the protection of Christ.

Winter Rest

In nature, everything beneath a wintery covering lays dormant, resting from Fall's thorough cleansing. As a result, plants, gardens, and animal inhabitants all gain a natural insulator against the frost and damaging winds with a soft blanket of snow. Yes, the stilling chilling snow is nature's insulator.

The quietness of a Winter season makes me want to dive back under the covers, light a warm fire, or grab a cup of tea and just gaze out over the beautiful blanket that falls from the Heavens. Layers of frozen rich nutrients arrive within every snowflake or raindrop from all across the globe, destined to nourish the sleeping soil beneath in [15]God's perfect timing. Peace lives in that regeneration process. Hope is clarified in an intimate inward experience of quietness with God. Your purpose is refined, and past pruning is reconciled in quiet maturing faith.

In this protective rest beneath the wintery blanket, there is a slow and steady melt that allows the Good News of Christ to trickle into your troubles, percolating through the trials, refilling you with peace, and providing matured faith for your nourishment and future needs.

Timing is an incredibly important part of seasonal change. If Winter's rest lingers too long, root systems can become a malnourished-soggy-unproductive mess beneath the covering. On the other hand, a perfect season of rest is beautifully designed to prepare us for the next season of purpose, so we've got to pay attention to the warning signs of a lingering rest or impending Winter storm. Seasons give themselves approximately three months per cycle. But these cycles can happen within us on the daily, even hourly.

Some seasons of rest may take longer than others, but if you rest in comfort longer than necessary, you can find yourself no longer productive in the particular gift set God was attempting to mature you in. Timing is very important, and we have to pay attention to the signs and warnings of something out of the ordinary happening within us.

---

[15] *. Ecclesiastes 3:1-8 (NIV)*

There is a time for everything, and a season for every activity under the heavens: a time to be born and a time to die, a time to plant and a time to uproot, a time to kill and a time to heal, a time to tear down and a time to build, a time to weep and a time to laugh, a time to mourn and a time to dance, a time to scatter stones and a time to gather them, a time to embrace and a time to refrain from embracing, a time to search and a time to give up, a time to keep and a time to throw away, a time to tear and a time to mend, a time to be silent and a time to speak, a time to love and a time to hate, a time for war and a time for peace.

We have become very advanced as a society at issuing Storm Warnings. They allow us to prepare ourselves for the possibility of chaos. We get internal and external warnings for impending life storms too. We just have to surround ourselves with experts that are willing to speak into our area of weakness. I have attempted to surround myself with a good balance of mentors, experts in the areas of life I need maturing. I balance that with mentees I may be able to assist when I see a storm moving in over their lives. Our society has created entire departments dedicated to identifying hazardous Winter signs and warnings. I'll bet you have a local body of believers, ready and willing to assist you too. They will help you identify areas you may need to rest in Christ's Peace for a season or two.

I don't need to be a civil engineer to recognize a Storm Warning is a serious warning, especially in urban areas, where orchards, vineyards, and people cannot handle extra heavy snow, freezing rain, or sleet. Tree limbs can snap in half from the sheer weight of a heavy snowfall. A rapid early melt can cause tremendous community chaos. In addition, the Good News of nourishment can easily become diverted runoff that picks up toxins, pollutants, and messes that make their way through an entire populous.

Know this: Not all chaos is created by God. We can call it to ourselves or receive the polluted runoff from someone else's Winter storm. Regardless of how we find ourselves in the chaos of Winter, we must still ourselves to let God do the work. Battling a Winter storm is generally not our battle to fight. They are His, and He is aware, standing between you and the enemy of your soul. There may be purpose in Him allowing it, and, in that case, the chaos is there to teach us to run to Him and rest in Him.

Chaos and Quietness

When God calls you into a season of rest,[16]be still, knowing God is God. Doubt if you must but at least run from indifference and prepare your heart to rest in God's strength rather than your own.

Distractions

So how then do we turn doubt, indifference, busyness, and movement over to God when a Winter season has arrived? Being still and [17]focusing our heart toward God is easier said than done when there are so many distractions vying for our attention.

Distractions (masquerading as purpose) can creep into seasons of rest and rob us of the very purpose we are shaped to accomplish in the seasons that follow. The more often I would resist a season of rest, the more often I would find myself thrust into it: [18]Divorce, illness, loss of a voice into something that truly mattered. Forced seasons of rest felt like the imprisonment of my mind, body, and soul. They were never God's intention for me to experience. [19]Choosing to rest in Him was the only peaceful way through those seasons.

---

[16] . *Psalm 46:10 New International Version (NIV) 10 He says, "Be still, and know that I am God; I will be exalted among the nations, I will be exalted in the earth."*

[17] . *Psalm 62:5 For God alone, O my soul, wait in silence, for my hope is from him.*

[18] . *Isaiah 30:1 (NIV) "Woe to the obstinate children," declares the Lord, "to those who carry out plans that are not mine, forming an alliance, but not by my Spirit, heaping sin upon sin;*

[19] . *Psalm 90:17 "May the favor of the LORD our God rest on us; establish the work of our hands for us- yes, establish the work of our hands"*

While writing this book about seasonal approaches to healing and purpose, I became distracted with anything other than the rest. God Called me to rest, but I figured I then had the time to write. The problem was I had no inspiration to write with. I wanted to finish the book. It had been dragging on for years, morphing into different messages with every rewrite. To me, writing meant purpose when there was nothing else to do, so I pushed on, pouring my energy onto paper, [20]hour after restless hour. The messages were chaotic and messy. None of my words made any sense. The more I moved, the more I struggled with clarity and purpose. I was becoming physically exhausted, yet my mind continued to entertain distractions.

For a strong entrepreneurial-spirited woman that wants every season to be the energetic Summer expression of who I am, resting was the last thing I thought I needed. I grew tired and frustrated to the point of almost giving up writing altogether. Resisting the forces of His nature, I had worked myself to a place and a feeling of exhausted-emptied-purposelessness. Finally, I gave my writing back to Him, and I rested.

I was laying in His arms, now face to face with my presupposition about who I thought I was, what the world said I was, wasn't, should, and shouldn't be. Once emptied of everything others expected of me, I came to terms with the truth of who I was in Christ. Emptied of myself completely, staring intimately into the face of God, I could see my own reflection there, which is exactly where I needed to be. My Winter's rest included removing something I enjoyed doing to create the space for something I was purposed to live.

Rest was revealing some hidden ugly truths about my motives for writing in the first place. Was I just going through the

---

[20]. *Isaiah 30:15 (NIV)This is what the Sovereign Lord, the Holy One of Israel, says: "In repentance and rest is your salvation, in quietness and trust is your strength, but you would have none of it.*

process of praying, scripture reading, journaling, wiping my tears while "saying" rather than "believing" the very things I wrote? Why was it that I'd choose anything but the silence when rest would call to me? The truth was, resting felt to me like being invisible and of no useful service. And until God emptied me of that lie, I would be of no useful service to the purpose I was called to write out on these pages. That was my Chaos of Quietness.

God's purpose for my life was often clarified in Winter's quietness with Him after the chaos.

Creating Storms of Chaos

Resisting rest has a chaotic way of turning a soft snowy Winter's blanket into a raging chaotic blinding blizzard. Even though God intently supervises me during those times, it still feels like an all hells broke loose type of chaos covering my life. The worst ones occur when I ignore the warnings. I'll quickly find myself unable to take one more step in any direction. I think Alaskans call them "whiteout storms." If a rope didn't tether me to God during those storms, I would be lost forever in them. If God does allow me to wander away, all I have to do is hang on to that rope. As I put one foot, one hand, in front of the other, I will eventually find my way back to the safety of His arms.

God is never the one who wanders off. I am. If I faithfully make my way back to Him, He is going to be right where I left Him. He will only allow me to wander so far as to bring us closer together again, but it has to be by my own free will.

Resisting His rest robs us both of the joy that comes from experiencing His peace, the kind God makes available to us only in Christ. Christ is the rope I am tethered to God with. When I am lost, wandering in a blinding Winter storm, that rope of Christ reminds me of His promises to me. He will use the pain of the season to strengthen and shape me and bring me full circle back to Him. Through each Winter storm, I learn to enjoy and trust the protective power of His peaceful quietness.

During the good seasons, I see the strengthening purpose behind God allowing chaos to exists at all in my life. My feet are firmly planted in the hope of the future while my head is still a questioning developer, and my heart strength is my belief in Christ to make everything work for good through every season. It is all part of my growth cycle with Him. Tethered to Him through each storm is how He allows me the latitude to work out my battles with Him. Even with my back turned, I'm still tethered to Him, and when the chaos passes, I've learned to trust His plan over my own. Those encounters have defined the outward expression of my life's purpose.

All those Winter seasons have brought me to this; Writing a book about lessons discovered during those seasons of chaos and quietness with God to help lead you to or back to Him through your unrest as well.

Purpose in Chaos

Knowing we can be in the center of a storm and still be under the protective power of His redemptive love may give us a new purpose for our chaos, don't you think? It may take a few seasons to find the redemptive value of the chaos in your life right now, but you'll find it because there is always purpose to our chaos if we are tethered to Christ in it.

God's purpose for our life is better than ours. He sees the entire cycle of seasons of our life as one whole picture. We experience seasons and chaos in minutes and hours. It's only in hindsight we see with wisdom the purpose of it all.

> **And with a Christian worldview, we can get a glimpse of his perfect plan moving forward too.**

The purpose of chaos can rest in the power of your prayer when you have no voice: the power of your faith walk when you are forbidden to move; the power of peaceful rest when the world is in chaos, and the power of God's redemptive regeneration in the face of evil.

God occupies that space between us and chaos, an intimately sacred space we share with God through the Holy Spirit's direction. Through moments filled with the complete stillness that requires surrender to be undisturbed, He is providing you with a purpose in this, His perfect process. It is intensely supervised by Him and necessary for a full body-mind-and-soul type of restorative-redeeming-growth process,

Chaos is good. Chaos is bad. Chaos is natural and neutral. So give it a rest— in Him.

Rest Needs Supervision

When my kids were growing up, quiet moments around my house were not to be trusted. Even now, as a grandparent, as long as there is noise in the house, I can pretty much discern where the kids are and what they are up to. It's when things get quiet that I bet the kids are up to, or into, something they probably need supervision over.

Whatever would bring my kids to a place of quiet in our home was usually intensely entertaining, adventurous, and quietingly captivating to them, maybe even dangerous for them if I left them unsupervised with it for long.

On the one hand, Christ-centered quietness has this same adventurous and quietingly captivating intensity to it. Because it captures attention and holds it like a whisper, it can be incredibly engaging, challenging, and filled with possibility. But, on the other hand, the quietness of a Winter rest can also turn boring or frustratingly painful to a restless-curious growing mind. The quietness of a Winter's chaos needs supervision.

When my granddaughter was younger, I would mandate a midday nap. The result of disturbing that restful peace, once I got her there, created chaos of the most difficult kind to manage later in the day: external for me and internal for her.

I imagine God sees our Winter season of rest in much the same way. He knows the healing we require from our rest with Him, and He is very protective of it when we submit to Him. He knows the potential we have to create chaos in the seasons ahead without it, so He requires us to rest for our growth, regeneration, recovery, maturity and help us live out the best version of ourselves on purpose with Him through the following seasons of our lives.

Newborns physically experience this seasonal regenerative cycle several times in a single day. Winter's rest is like nap time for recovery, then Spring feeding for nourishment, Summer play for expenditure, and a good Fall cleansing comes with a

Chaos and Quietness

diaper change. Then back we go to a sweet Winter's rest, over and over again throughout the day.

As adults, our physical bodies will go through this cycle every seven years or so. As we age, the process may begin to slow down a bit as seasons begin to stretch out over longer periods. But, they are still part of the physical process of life. It can be mid-summer on nature's calendar when a metaphorical Winter's rest calls you to awareness.

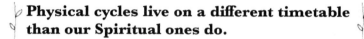

Physical cycles live on a different timetable than our Spiritual ones do.

God's written Word gives us cycles to consider: [21]Creation, [22]Salvation, [23]Eternity. These are just a few found in His Word. In your rest and quiet time with Him, ask Him to speak to you about the spiritual maturity cycle you may be in right now. It's fun to let nature point us back to the Creator, but don't miss the opportunity to mature in the Truth of His Word once you are quieted with Him. Be aware of your cycle.

My oldest grandchild was remarkably aware of her surroundings as a newborn, almost hyper-interested in all that was going on around her. She didn't want to miss a thing. I'd be rocking her into that quite restful place of full body and mind surrender

---

[21] . *Genesis 1:1-31 ESV In the beginning, God created the heavens and the earth. The earth was without form and void, and darkness was over the face of the deep. And the Spirit of God was hovering over the face of the waters. And God said, "Let there be light," and there was light. And God saw that the light was good. And God separated the light from the darkness. God called the light Day, and the darkness he called Night. And there was evening and there was morning, the first day.*

[22] . *John 14:6 "I am the way, the truth, and the life: no man cometh unto the Father, but by Me"*

[23] . *Revelation 14:11 ESV And the smoke of their torment goes up forever and ever, and they have no rest, day or night, these worshipers of the beast and its image, and whoever receives the mark of its name."*

when all of a sudden, she would arch her back like an acrobat and push away from my chest just so she could get a glimpse of the wind blowing on the curtain panels behind us.

Aware and interested in every little thing that caught her attention, pushing boundaries and laughing at the possibility of it all, she often reminded me of myself. I much preferred the idea of playtime with God rather than resting during many of my Winter Seasons. So I would do this kind of dance on ice with God when I should have been resting. First, I would venture out on cracking ice, never knowing the thickness yet aware of the distinct crackling sounds it made when venturing too far. Then I would laugh and squeal at the adventure, completely disregarding the danger of it all, trusting that strong grip God had on my life would hold me up, just as my grandchild would do in my arms as a baby.

Often it would be necessary to tighten my grip around my granddaughter's little waist to keep her from falling out of my arms, and each time I did, she would push against me even harder and arch her back even further. That child had no idea she could really get hurt if I let go of her in those moments of struggle. I'd grab on to whatever flailing limb I could catch to keep from dropping her onto her head, all the while ignoring her breath-holding or ear-piercing screeches to have things her own way, just as I would do to God when He was calling me in off the ice for a Winters rest. He lovingly endures my resistance just as I would endure the struggle with my sweet grandbaby, simply to hang on to her for her own good.

I get that kid, though. My protective, stilling embrace probably felt like restrictive chaos to her, the kind I naturally want to fight and push back on when I should be resting too. But ultimately, her struggle, as is mine, is futile. The end result is that grandchild will eventually find herself at rest in my arms. And more times than not, it is from sheer exhaustion.

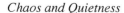

That is what it's like to fight a season of rest called into our life by God. He will use any opportunity, grab hold of us and keep us from falling on our heads, or in my case, through the ice, for as long as it takes. We can fight it only for so long, but eventually, we will tire, and in exhaustion, we collapse in His arms where He can safely carry us into our next season with Him.

From an outsider's perspective, those struggling moments with my grandkids probably looked quite chaotic. I knew exactly what I was doing with her, but an onlooker couldn't possibly know her as intimately as I do. To me, the chaos was simply a part of the maturing process of our time together. Even today, the older and stronger she gets, the more difficult it is to keep her from slipping away. But I've learned through the past struggles to simply hold on through the chaos no matter how long it takes.

The same is true for you and me. No matter how chaotic the world appears to us or the struggle appears to the world, God knows what He is doing. Always encouraging, always guiding, and always holding on to us. Chaos can rage—and in this world, it will. It's coming for us: a time where a worldly shout will call us out of our season of rest, even suggest we do not rest at all. The chaos will lure us out onto thin ice just for the excitement of watching us drown in our own loneliness and self-loathing. But we must rest, and our rest needs supervision. In Christ, we are never alone. No matter how chaotic our season may appear to others, there is purpose in the chaos. There is purpose in the call to come in off the ice and simply rest.

After The Struggle

The struggles I faced as a parent and revisiting as a grandparent has taught me to look for precious peace after the struggles. Kids eventually become exhausted of the struggle (as do we), the screeches end (as ours will), and the chaos of distractions pass (ours will too). When those moments happened for me and my littles, I could see it in their face. Peace. That regenerative surrender of quietness would fill the room except for the sound of my humming. My little wiggle worm would move her little head toward my heart., because against my chest, she could hear the deep vibrations of her favorite melody I would be humming for her good pleasure: "You are my Sunshine," "Jesus Loves You," and Walt Disney's "A Dream." She'd tuck her little arm up under my hair and around my neck and stare me intently in the face. She had to get to the place where she was completely emptied of her own movement and noise to recognize my sweet sounds, the ones that brought her joy. Then she'd snuggle in ever closer, trusting it was safe in my arms, exchanging her will for the safety of my rocking and song.

Winter's rest requires us to do much of the same. Struggle if you must, but eventually, you will begin to trust the peace that comes with exchanging your will for the safety of His rocking and song. Whatever familiar sound it is for you, you'll know it when you hear it, but you must move in close to Him and listen. When you are in His grasp, listening to His melody pouring out over your life, the entire world could crumble around you, and it wouldn't matter. You know you are safe, cared for, and protected.

Learning to rest in Christ today equips us for tomorrow's storms. Respond to this day's chaos so you are better equipped for the chaos ahead. Storms are coming. Big ones. Storms that will quiet your voice and disturb your soul. It's only in His grasp you will find comfort, hope, purpose, redemption, and peace.

Peace is found on the other side of the struggle. When you are been called to a season of rest, [24]rest in Him.

For His Good Pleasure

The struggles to get my kids to that perfect place of rest were some of my greatest challenges, followed by the sweetest memories of motherhood. My kid's restful submissions were always marked by an unmistakable sound from parted perfect little lips as a lung full of air was gently released with a sigh. Arms would go soft, and those little bodies were fully at rest in my arms. Those moments were turning point lessons for them and a satisfyingly encouraging experience for me.

In those moments, I could carry my children as far away from the chaos as I wanted them to go or simply stay there and rest a while with them, protecting them, speaking life over them and into their future. "I got you, little button," I'd whisper and lean in to kiss the crown of their little head and pray over them as they slept. "What do you need?" I'd whisper as my eyes surveyed them from head to toe in that perfect resting state.

When we can hear the gentle vibrations of God's heartbeat, we recognize the comfort of the tune. So take a moment, look up amid your Winter suffering. Calm yourself and give into

---

[24] . Matthew 11:28,29,30 "Come to me, all you who are weary and burdened, and I will give you rest. Take my yoke upon you and learn from me, for I am gentle and humble in heart, and you will find rest for your souls. For my yoke is easy and my burden is light."

His embrace. By intently looking for Christ's peace amid your chaos, you'll begin to rest. His Word of hope has been reverberating throughout the world in Christ for over two thousand years. Christ is what you need.

If you are serving Him in some capacity right now, and you have been called to a season of rest, remember, we delight Him more in resting with Him than in serving Him during a metaphorical Winter's rest. You may want to run to "serve and do" but, He beckons you to calm yourself within his grasp first.

Perhaps He has shaped you to run and jump and go and do, but it is in these chaotically quiet moments of rest, He will shape you to go and do those things even better for [25]His Good Pleasure in the Spring season ahead.

And now, Spring is here!

---

[25] . *Philippians 2:13 (ESV) "For it is God who works in you, both to will and to work for his good pleasure.*

~Spring~

Chaos & Quietness of Spring

"May the God of hope fill you with all joy and peace as you trust in him, so that you may overflow with hope

by the power of the Holy Spirit."

Romans 15:13 NIV

Hope/Planning

We are coming out of a Winter's rest and into the light of a joy-filled, energetic Spring season. Time to wake up!

Spring is a time to prepare for the goodness on its way with proper care of the day's gifts. Spring trees are busy absorbing nutrients found in their surrounding soil. They need proper nutrients to bud. So do we! Spring is our time to get our hands dirty, so to speak, by digging around in the soil we are planted in. We can learn from nature, so as we learn through Spring what nutrients are found in our life's soil, we want to understand God's timing over our ability to absorb His nutrient-rich Word—and that takes patience.

Could you imagine the quiet hours of chaos required to watch a fruit-bearing tree grow minute by minute? Unfortunately, I think we often judge our lives based solely on seeing results (fruit) rather than appreciating the growth processes that get us there.

Among the manure-laden trees amid the garden, I see faith-building hope-signals that fruit is actually being produced through this growing season, even though I cannot see the actual fruit itself. Most of my favorite fruits don't even appear until Summer, but Spring is where I'm most reminded that goodness is on the way:

Signs like early buds developing on long skinny tree limbs.

The sounds of birds utilizing twigs to prepare nests near the promised abundance soon to arrive.

The Spring rains stirring the sweet scents of early blooms.

And while we can only appreciate the fruit itself in its proper season, those early signals stimulate a hope-filled plan within us, hope that the future seasons' abundance is indeed beginning now.

Hope is the essence of Spring! Now is a great time to evaluate the source (or soil) from which you are drawing your life-giving, fruit-building potential. Take a moment to answer these questions as best you can. You may be surprised at what you find hiding in your soil.

- What is coming alive in you?
- What kinds of blooms (beginnings) do you see now or hope to see in the future?

- What type of fruit (results) are you hoping for in the season ahead?
- Are the desired fruits of your life in line with truth statements about you that are life-giving and true?
- Here is an even messier question: How do you know if what you are telling yourself—about yourself— is true, fruitful, and life-giving?

Dig around in the soil of your life and identify the life-giving nutrients. But, unfortunately, core beliefs grounded in anything other than unchanging Truths add a slow poison, rather than a fertilizer, to the soil of your life-giving and receiving process.

Truth is our life's fertilizer, but what exactly is TRUTH? How do you recognize it? Where can you find it? Who will share it with you if you don't have any? And if someone does share their life-giving fertilizer with you, how can you know if that truth is authentic, life-giving truth for you?

Consider this:

> **Life-giving, unchangeable truth offers consistent hope that the fruit buds of your life will bear a sweet-smelling aroma, even when you realize your buds may not flower in this particular season.**

Truth works like a Hope-fertilizer. Truth offers "consistent nutrition like hope encourages us to persevere. It's not temporary or seasonal but sustaining and fortifying.

Even though a fruitless season can look and even feel like a chaotic waste of season for sure, but hope offers you a quiet peace in the chaos until the season runs its course.

So, if you are having difficulty finding peace in the waiting of a chaotic season, you may need to add a little more hope-fertilizer to your life.

It is Faith-building to "experience" hope in a non-flowering or non-fruitful Spring season, but it's easy to confuse hope and faith. I don't want to get ahead of myself by talking about faith just yet, though. So let's stay focused on truth, hope, and growth for just a bit longer.

So, what happens if you find you lack a little hope in your soil? A lack of hope is a signal to you that you have stopped growing in some way! But the good news is that once you realize you have stopped growing in some way, you can more easily recognize you lack an abundance of enduring hope somehow.

 A lack of hope is simply a signal.

I have often felt the most hopeless chaos right before my most significant moments of growth because the chaos of stagnation (no growth, fruitlessness) is a sign to nourish myself in unchanging truth that brings life-sustaining hope.

Think of it this way: When you are thirsty, your body gives you a signal, and you desire water. When you are hungry, your belly grumbles to remind you to eat something. Likewise, lack of hope creates chaos, and chaos is a sign that you need more hope for a life-giving fruitful season. Hope (little h) alone is neither all good nor all bad. It's just necessary. But if you're adding hope on the daily and you're still in the midst of chaos with no peace and no growth, you may be lacking "life sustaining-*Truth*-filled-hope.'

Perhaps your spirit is thirsty. Find out if what you have placed your hope in is eternally fruitful Truth. Do you need Spiritual nourishment?

If your spirit is thirsty, your soul is hungry, and your heart will be longing for God's purpose to be revealed in your life. Chaos can bring your attention to a faith-filled seasonal process of intentionally adding Truth filled-Hope-building nutrients back into your life.

Spring cycles return over and over, each with new opportunities to absorb. Some Spring seasons are spent making personal growth plans, while others are appropriately spent absorbing the nutrients of faith-building. Chaos stirs things up and offers room in your soil to move out the toxins while adding hope-building eternally life-giving Truth-filled nutrients back to your soil.

Maybe it's time to consider a new story about what the process of chaos is all about. Do you want to know how to add Truth filled, eternal hope-building fertilizer to your faith-growing experiences that will ensure fruitful outcomes throughout each cycle?

Hard Questions

As this particular chapter unfolds, you may find yourself restless, even impatient about possible limiting beliefs you'll discover that have been holding you back. As you end this chapter, you'll be approaching some even more complex questions that I pray you will have the strength to dig into. But get messy anyway. You'll never regret this process.

Spring is the best time to suck up all the best nutrients you can get. When viewing the circumstances of your life, let hope neutralize the negative feelings or actions those negative feelings may have been producing.

It's time to rewrite your story with hope as the author of your core beliefs about you and your life. It isn't always easy to do, but well worth the effort. Because of the hopeless story my childhood had written across my heart, I allowed myself to believe things that were limiting to my growth cycle as I grew year after year. Then I'd become bitter about the fact that I didn't see fruit for my efforts during those fruitless seasons.

My life-fruits were toxic and had become a chaotic process of perfectionism that I had set in motion to survive my seasons rather than thrive in them. Season after season, I'd be looking for and waiting upon the life-giving fruits to bloom. Some Springs, I'd get some buds, but in my chaos, I'd strip those possibilities down by my own hand. "Not good enough," I'd shout in my chaos!

Eventually, I got tired of doing hard work with no fruit-bearing results and decided to do the more challenging work of letting in hope. Hope is where the quietness came amid my chaos—allowing hope to tell me a *new story* about the circumstances of my life that weren't negative and limiting allowed a proper nourishing cycle to feed my root system. The fruit didn't bloom right away, but I felt something happening that was new and filled me with peace. I was less focused on the outcome, and for several seasons I focused on evaluating the core beliefs (fertilizer of my life) I was operating from. Once I realized I hadn't been absorbing truth-filled faith-building nutrients of hope, I dug in even deeper and eventually found peace-filled, fruitful thriving.

Hope allowed me to let go of perfectionism to make room for new growth and new budding opportunities. What I once wanted was seeming less desirable as new purposes for my life were made more apparent. Season after season, hope grew, and my "Faith."

And it all started with a little truthful digging around in the dirt and adding hope. And, now I know where to find the best source of it!

HOPE

Fruit trees don't require hope to survive each season. Instead, they respond to the seasonal processes without choice, so an actual tree has no use for hope and faith. But nature's fruit cycles make for great story metaphors up to the point of choice-making.

See you and me; we do have the choice. We have free will to choose where and what we place our fruit-budding, faith-filling hope in. But, what's more, we develop our faith by what we place our hope in and develop our hope with what we place our faith in, season after season.

Make no mistake, YOU NEED HOPE, and when I say, "you NEED hope," I mean we literally require it. We can't remain alive long without it. We can go maybe 40 days without food, three days without water, perhaps eight minutes without air. But without hope, there is no survival unless there is intervention.

Psychogenic death is a real thing. It isn't suicide, and it isn't linked to depression. It's the act of giving up on life. It is almost the opposite of surrendering in hope-filled faith. Psychogenic death (for lack of hope) is a very real physical condition according to a study published in US News by Dr. John Leach, author and research fellow at the University of Portsmouth. "Motivation is essential for coping with life, and if that fails," Leach says, "apathy is almost inevitable." Yet even the most apathetic condition is reversible with a little faith-filled, hopeful intervention.

Now, I'm a Jesus girl, so I'm about to liken Jesus to a nourishing, truth-filled-hope- renewing-life-fertilizer sent from God. Faith in Jesus is a great hope-generator but so much more than just survival or fruit growing. It is chaos-quieting and eternal life-giving!

Hope always follows faith, and faith generates more hope. They are intimately connected, yet Scripture tells us they also remain separate. (1 Corinthians 13:13 says this: "Now these three remain: faith, hope, and love…"). They are separate so that they are not vulnerable to our storms and chaos as a whole, yet connected to help us grow through them. We can get through one season with little faith and lots of hope and another with lots of faith and a little hope that way. I've done it. I know!

All of life's fruit-filled tomorrows insist on some measure of hope. Hope knows stuff we don't. It brings things together and makes seasons work as one. It's the perfect fertilizer for your particular growth process. Hope attracts necessary things, beautiful, sweet-smelling miraculous things, energetic things, life-giving-chaos-suddenly disappearing kinds of things. Hope is what motivates us to think higher, live upward, and blossom. Blossoms are the expressions of our hope and faith in our very lives.

The purpose to which we've been born is to use our time, talent, and treasures for good and glorify God!

With hope alive, faith blooms, and when faith is in full bloom, it's a spectacular season, to be sure.

The Process

A beautiful fruit-filled life is a growing process. Fruit doesn't just grow atop the dirt, leaving nothing for the season ahead, and it certainly requires something from the season behind. Healthy, vibrant, sweet fruit takes time to develop. The same can be said of hope and faith-building maturity cycles. Each season benefits from the previous by providing for the next. Nature uses Spring as a time to absorb nutrients from the ground to prepare for buds and blooms.

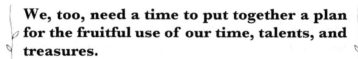

> **We, too, need a time to put together a plan for the fruitful use of our time, talents, and treasures.**

When was the last time you considered the purpose of your life's unique fruiting design? You have a personality shaped by experiences and talents you were born with and abilities you have learned over the years. You even have fruitful gifts to use for the blessing of others.

Blossoms are always a great indicator of fruit to come, but the fruit itself (time, talents, and treasures) is the end result of years of nourishing maturity cycles.

Did you know that a seed-started tree can take up to 10 years to produce fruit? That's up to 40 seasons of quiet, non-fruit-bearing chaos to bloom purposefully in just one season. I bet you're feeling pretty good about your own life's fruit in light of that little nugget, but it gets even better. Over the lifetime of that very tree, it can have almost 100 opportunities to bloom through a 100-year cycle. Now that's the kind of fruit worth waiting for.

Thank heavens we aren't a tree, but metaphorically speaking, consider how [26] sweet-smelling our blooms can be when infused with the kind of hope and faith we get through numerous cycles of chaotic and quiet maturity-building processes!

Spring-Loading Spring

A happy mind makes way for a happy body. When we are trying to build hope upon things that require faith to understand, it's always a good idea to start with the proper nutrition of the mind and body. It takes energy to support a healthy mindset for the framing of a fruitful life's plan. Get a head start on your Spring thinking by leveraging the high mineral content found in abundance in the green leafy vegetables of a Spring garden. Try juicing them for physical healing and regeneration.

Healing can happen quite rapidly by juicing spring greens. Depending on what part of the world you live in, Spring greens contain nutrients that can neutralize the acid in your body. An alkaline environment is what the mind mostly prefers. Spring greens can grow in abundant varieties, creating all kinds of alkaline-forming foods that can be plucked fresh from your garden. They will put a little extra spring in your step (excuse the pun) and give you a head start on all the planning Spring will require of you.

---

[26] . *Ephesians 5:2 "Walk in love, even as Christ also loved you, and gave himself up for us, an offering and a sacrifice to God for a sweet-smelling fragrance."*

But we can't juice hope, right? Hope must be consumed through the spirit, where it enters into the heart and alkalinizes the brain and body. The alkalinizing nutrients of hope and faith must be fully received into the heart through the reading of His Word to be of any fruitful use long term.

"Biblical Hope" is like concentrated amounts of acid-neutralizing, peace-forming nutrients. Biblical hope is different from the world's ever-changing kind of acid-producing hope. Biblical **hope** is built on [27]faith in Jesus and Jesus alone. Biblical **faith** is a twofer. It can serve as a chaos-creating intellectual asset and our emotional peace-filled security blanket of quiet **hope** at the same time. Biblical **faith** is like having the proper fertilizer that guarantees eternal blooms and fruitfulness.

Metaphorically speaking, our Springs of life are when we want to read the ingredients on our life's fertilizer bag. No matter how much faith you put in a fertilizer bag marked "Fruit and Blossom Poison," it's still poison! A fruitful life will not grow from that nutrient.

> **Get the fertilizer wrong, and everything is affected negatively.**

You have to know your fertilizer, understand the application steps as it relates to your life and circumstances, appreciate the proper doses for the season you're in, and give yourself plenty of time to absorb all the fertilizing goodness. That messy, even smelly chaos is going to produce the most beautiful life-giving flowers and fruit in the seasons to come. So quiet the chaos and enjoy the process.

---

[27] . *Titus 2:13* "Looking for that blessed hope, and the glorious appearing of the great God and our Savior Jesus Christ;"

The Analysis

So, let's do it now. Let's get a Spring season going in your life. Let's analyze the components of the nutrients you are drawing your hope and faith from.

- Where are you placing your faith?
- What hope do you have because of your faith?

Okay, now let's dig even deeper into that Spring soil of your life. This is the getting-your-hands-dirty-deep-down-in-the-manure-smell-like-you-need-a-shower-hard-questions- you have to ask yourself about Christ. Because getting to know Him is like any other relationship. It takes effort and work. It takes seasons of development.

If you really want to understand the chaos, now is the best time to prepare yourself for it. Will you find parasites and poison in your soil that need to be removed? Do it now. Prepare to be elbow deep in a big muddy mess as you dig around here in silence. Below are some Jesus girl "scriptural questions" I want you to dig around in. It is here, in this muddy chaos, that faith comes alive. Enjoy this process.

Forget about fruit, successes, and failures for a moment. Instead, just concentrate on the discovery process. It will get easier as you go. God understands everything you question, yet He is un-reducible by His nature, so go ahead, ask away of Him. Hope and faith are tucked into knowing that; *He is who He says He is and will do what He said He will do*! If we find we are confident in what we have placed our hope in, every moment, be it chaotic, quiet, or euphoric, will be purposeful and life-giving.

Spring-Time Fertilizing Scriptural Questions:

- [28]Do you completely trust Jesus for your eternal destiny?
- [29]Do you trust that His death was substituted for your sin?
- [30]Do you believe the death and resurrection of His body was provided by a loving God for YOUR personal salvation[31] and is available to anyone by faith?
- [32]Do you believe you are forgivable?
- [33]Do you trust Jesus' words when He said He is coming again?

As a Jesus girl myself, my prayer is you answered yes to all of the above questions. If so, this Spring season of hope requires you to continue the work by answering each question with a, "how deeply do you…?"

It is here you begin to *mature* your faith, which reveals the purpose of your unique fruiting design. If you said, "I don't

---

[28] . Romans 5:8 But God demonstrates his love toward us, in that while we were still sinners, Christ died for us'

[29] . Romans 3:23 For all have sinned and fall short of the Glory of God'

[30] . John 3:16 For God so loved the world, that He gave His only begotten Son, that whoever believes in Him should not perish but have everlasting life›

[31] . Romans 10:13 "For whoever calls on the name of the LORD shall be saved"

[32] . Acts 2:38 "Repent, and let every one of you be baptized in the name of Jesus Christ for the remission of sins; and you shall receive the gift of the Holy Spirit"

[33] . John 14:3 (KJV) And if I go and prepare a place for you, I will come again, and receive you unto myself; that where I am, [there] ye may be also.

know," are you feeling weary? Are you at a place where your yes's have turned to "I don't know?" It's okay. Just take the time now to re-nourish your relationship with Christ. Checking up on your fertilizer may mean stepping back from the religion, the system, the program, toxic people, places, and things.

Seasons of rest and letting the Holy Spirit regenerate me with the nutrients I didn't even know I needed is what helped me quiet the chaos of my fruitless Springs. Let Christ's life-giving words regenerate you. You'll see your relationship with yourself and others become more peace-filled almost immediately. The fertilizing truth God established before time beneath the soil of your growth is all there. You just have to dig for it, sit with it, and build upon it. These messy, chaotic efforts will bear fruit in the seasons ahead.

Suppose you said NO to any of the above questions, and you are experiencing chaos right now. In that case, the Spring season of your "Biblical hope" lies in the journey of discovering why you said No and figuring out where your hope-fertilizer is actually coming from.

What truths have you accepted as life-giving that are actually sucking the life out of you?

Jesus gave us this promise: "Because I live, you also will live" (John 14:19).

Have you let someone or something steal your peace? Are you feeling dead inside? Is there a part of your life that is grey and decaying? An acidic environment is a chaotic environment. If your information comes from the acid-soaked grounds of a toxic waste plant, what do you think that will do to your life-giving fruit cycle in seasons to follow? The thief of your peace is like the toxic waste of this world. God is not the Creator of destruction, yet He will allow it if you choose that for yourself.

But I pray you will fortify yourself with supplementation that will lead you back to a truth-filled relationship with Christ. When a tree is rooted in acidic toxic waste, it needs to be supplemented with healthy, viable nutrients even to stand a chance of growth. If it is malnourished, it will begin to break down. When WE are malnourished, we begin to break down. Toxins seep in, and disease (dis-ease) is soon to follow. Hope can still live, but it's much more challenging to thrive in a toxic environment when you are already weakened without healing nutrients to supplement your life's plan.

The closer we get to formulating a plan to live out our purpose and calling utilizing our unique fruiting design, the harder the Enemy of our soul will try to silence and poison the environment around us. Just look at the world today. I began writing this book in 2015. It is now 2021, and the seasons of this world's decay and poison are stronger than ever. Poison is hidden in plain sight. Actually, as of 2020, I noticed it is not even hidden anymore. Evil is served up as the norm. It hurts my soul. I can't even watch entertainment channels any longer without seeing poisonous propaganda shoved in my face.

But Jesus was the healing supplement I needed long before my eyes fell upon the poisonous additives of this world. The Enemy prowls, God protects. Chaos is universal, but God is bigger than the universe. So I say [34]pay no attention to what the world is saying, doing, or not doing. Don't be afraid. Pay no attention to death. Live! Live in the chaos. Live through the chaos. Live beyond the chaos. Live despite the chaos. Christ is the world's poison antidote! Your chaos will lead you deeper into transformational peace, growth, and faith in Christ if you choose it. Don't resist it. We have His Holy Spirit to equip us in our struggles. He aims to pull us closer, direct our steps,

---

[34] . *Mark 5:36 Overhearing what they said, Jesus told him, "Don't be afraid; just believe."*

guide us, clarify our purpose, and develop His character in our labor and living.

Scripture tells us that [35]this world is not our home, so there will be things that just won't sit right with us. And trust me when I say I see many things these days that just don't sit right with me. But the Springs of my relationship with Christ are like alkaline to an acidic body. This world has gotten almost too acidic to understand, live, and thrive in. But my past chaos has made it easier for me to say no to more chaos because Christ has come that we may live a [36]full life now, and into eternity.

This world is chaotic, but for me, it is neither good nor bad for my soil any longer. My fertilizer is Christ, and Christ is neutralizing the chaos, quieting the chaos, and using it for good. Because of Him, I get to see God stand between my chaos and quietness, protecting and creating with it. Season after season. Every hour, every minute, a new storm forms on the horizon, threatening to wash the world's poisons my way, and God is there at the creation of it, to meet it before it washes over me with its toxic residues.

God stands between you and Satan too. God says He will fight to the death for you. He has fought to the death for you— in Christ. He died for you! You never have to fight a hopeless death battle again. It has been won!

With Christ, you can truly know that you know "you know," you are no longer fighting chaos for your life?! In Christ, our chaos is used to bring us toward Eternal life. Death no longer serves a purpose for chaos. There is no need any longer, my friend, to fight a battle that has already been won for you. Meeting

---

[35] *. Hebrews 13:4 (NIV) For this world is not our permanent home; we are looking forward to a home yet to come.*

[36] *. John 10:10 NIV The thief comes only to steal and kill and destroy; I have come that they may have life, and have it to the full.*

chaos like that is just depressing and un-endurable. But when you have chaos and thrive with Christ through it, He seems to have a way of equipping us with added clarity to strategize and fight for the territory we have already been given.

For this Spring cycle, why not let God lead. He knows you personally. He cares who you are and is passionately protective of you, especially during a Spring cycle when you are drawing nearer to Him. You can take His love personally and count on Him to reveal as much truth about Himself as you can absorb. Chaos will soon become less and less annoying, and your life's toxic runoff is reduced to a compost pile. He will turn your messes into nutrients in the seasons to come. God comes to us in Christ and is with us in the Holy Spirit, always fighting for us and in us. God does not offer you "everything you want" just to get compliance from you, yet he will give you every nutrient you ask according to His will. He will use any song, person, situation, or season to sincerely guide you to deeper unshakable truth in Him.

To truly live life to the fullest, in this life and the next means to start living right now! Right where you are. Do not hesitate, rationalize, or try to find a self-satisfying solution to your situation. Think eternally! Think bigger than your circumstances! Think outside of the chaos, and you'll soon see freedom—the forever-ever kind.

Join me and thousands—maybe millions—of others being encouraged right now by reading the stories of Timothy in the Bible. Paul is an excellent example of an encourager to Timothy in the face of opposition and chaos of the time. Perhaps like me, you have been called to be an encourager to others? Make the simple choice of mind to go from being a hostage of your chaos to a healer with stories of your perseverance through it!

Equip His Saints?

If your story of perseverance was the truth-supplementation another person suffering in chaos needed to keep them from drinking in the toxins of this world, wouldn't you want to share that truth with them? That kind of wisdom is not out there to be revealed. It's already been shared with you. Take the opportunity to formulate a Spring plan to release your gift of wisdom into the world. In doing so, together, as God saves us, we help make sense of the chaos for others and perhaps spare them unbearable, even unnecessary, burdens.

When I was very young, God told me I would be used to "equip his saints." I had no idea what that meant or how to process that information. I simply remember giving my life to Christ through a TV Evangelism show while babysitting one evening. I was about 12. I cried. The guy on the TV held out his hand, and somehow I was now a part of Christ's family, which I understood very little about. I didn't have the tools, nor was I surrounded by people to help me understand what being a part of Christ's family really meant. I had simply chosen to be "IN."

So, from that moment on, Spring's regenerative process was "available" to me. Still, my places of encouragement and nourishment were so toxic and chaotic that I rarely wanted to be "in them." I set about life preferring to be "out there," doing something rather than waiting for something to come to me. That personality got wired into my DNA, so God provided the kind of chaos with just enough spiritual nourishment mixed in to require more than just "me" to experience Him fully. But once I got it, I couldn't help but want to share the Good News in every way I could.

Seriously, I'm a terrible speller and really poor with grammar, so the last thing I imagined God would give me to equip and encourage His saints while glorifying Him was writing. Yet, here I am, and here you are. Yes, that would be *you*, a saint in need of equipping. If you are reading this book and made it this far into this particular chapter, I'm certain you are a saint He wants equipped and encouraged. He is speaking to you, my friend.

With each Spring season, God provides relationships to both strengthen us and quiet life's noise. He uses people differently-abled than us to walk with us, sit with us, run with us, hold us still, hold us down, lift us up, and encourage us to go, each one acting as catalysts to the next, nourishing our spiritual soil and cultivating our willingness to "grow" where He sends us.

Every significant life value I have revisited during a Spring regeneration has provided insights that changed how I looked at my future circumstances and gave me clarity in purpose with compassion to lead forward. I'd find confidence, significance, and freedom from the quietness or the chaos and grow more faith-filled. My past chaos was always destined to be used for good somehow.

During my vocational leadership years, those years in which I was purposed to lead others well, I spent several Spring seasons asking good questions and digging around in the soil I had been planted in. I'll share some of the questions I asked myself during those early years here. Perhaps they can prove useful and nutrient-rich for you, too, if you should find yourself in such a position.

As a purposed leader, I had chosen to allow God to use me to lead others in an organized fashion toward community and maturity in Christ. But I have to say, so many nights, I'd go home asking more questions of God than He was answering.

Some seasons He seemed quiet altogether. Those were some of the most terrifying, chaotic seasons of my life. Until I understood that it was in His quietness, He spoke to me the loudest and most clearly. Once I began to rely on Christ to work through me instead of me working for Christ, well, the chaos of that kind of quietness became peaceful, and my ability to encourage and truly lead others from persevering in faith grew bold, loud, and clear.

Some of these questions may stir you and challenge you. Others may help you to let go to formulate a new plan. Both are positive nutrients if properly added to your Spring leadership regeneration process. See if any of them resonate with you.

- Is what I'm asking others to do, or am I doing myself, *aligned with my values* and life goals?
- Is what I am planning to do, or planning for others to participate in, serving to *glorify God or me*?
- Are my goals and plans *showing love* to others, blessing them somehow, or equipping them?
- What will our team or I need to *be prepared to sacrifice* should we need to push through some chaos?
- Do I have all the resources I need to push a chaotic agenda if called upon?
- Is this the right season to lead through the chaos with confidence? Will I need additional skills?
- On the way to accomplishing the goals I've set before my team, wherein the journey might chaos come up, and where have I created peace-bridges to rest and regenerate the team along the way?
- Would I be standing on an incline or a decline if I faced massive chaos and choose to push on through?
- What has created that potential chaos in the past?

- Has someone already figured out how to push on through that kind of chaos, and do I have access to them?
- And one of the most important questions I ever asked myself during my vocational leadership years was: Is this my chaos to be pushing on through in the first place, or should I be moving in a different direction altogether?

Knowing whether to push, when to push harder, when to push through and if I should push at all gives faith room to work in the chaos should you choose to move ahead during those seasons. Pushing on through chaos you have positively identified as yours to push on through allows hope room to generate more faith because you know the effort is not going to be in vain. I love seeing chaos simply fade away even as sweat is dripping down my brow. Faith, Hope, and Love regenerate, nourish, and provides the energy needed to take us right up those hills, through the valleys, and into the next season with joy, no matter the visible fruits.

The power of Springs spent in the company of other Christians going in the same direction goes far beyond our understanding of space and time. If you overcome any resistance to move closer to Christ, the energy you generate from that choice alone will become gloriously unstoppable!

Storm Cycles

In the past, I'd often get caught up in some chaos that would make me forget how intimately God loves me in Christ. I'd want to run away from the chaos and run to be with "Him" at the sea or the top of a mountain. Almost as if "in the distance" is where God lives. Over there. Far from me. Big. Ominous and removed. Then in comes a big, thundering storm: lightning bolts, floods, the works. Eventually, I'd find myself running back to the safety of knowing Christ intimately.

Today I know Jesus personally. I trust He is who He says He is and will always do what He says he will do. But perhaps my eyes see what others can't comprehend without knowing Jesus, so I have found nature is a great place to find His glory to share.

So, imagine with me if you will God looking out over our lives like we would look out over a great forest from a mid-mountain view. Our eyes would see the entire range as one picture in our mind. And that's because from that view we can only see the tops of the trees. We might imagine what was going on below the thick fog layer and makeup stories in our minds about what we think is happening, but we can't know for sure because we can only see the entire canopy as one.

God sees humanity in much the same way, yet God sees clearly down through the canopy, down past the covering, and right into our inner branches. He sees the broken and the dead ones, the flowering and the fruitful. He sees the future fawn that will come to feed on the green foliage beneath the tree's branches. He sees the massive tangled root system, rotting and renewing. He sends in the microscopic organisms to return what we would call dead back into nutrient-rich life.[37] He sees every detail of who you are and knows you personally.

While much the same way, the dead 'dis-eased' parts of our life can be regenerated and used by God to inspire others if we are brave enough to share our trials and victories.

---

[37]. *Your eyes saw my unformed substance; in your book were written, every one of them, the days that were formed for me, when as yet there was none of them. Ps 139:16*

He will even use the storms of our life to wash away with surging rains, that which no longer serves a purpose. Storms are often how God sends nutrients past the beautiful canopies that others see and directly to our root systems, where we need hydration and nourishment.

In the beginning, it was often all I could do during a storm just to stand still and wait upon the Lord to shower me with goodness. I was learning to trust, but I'd often close my eyes in faith to believe while the wind whipped around me. Eventually, I learned just to take a deep breath, open my eyes, and lean into the chaos. Each time I found God was there within me, holding me up, moving me forward, or sheltering me while I stood still. He is within me during the storms and within me during His whispers. Why? Because Jesus is alive IN me.

How odd that He would love me enough to open a place inside of me where my roots will go deeper into Him, deep enough to secure me through any storm or mountain of chaos. Eventually, I began to notice Him in the little things all around me as well. Not Holy Spirit indwelled inanimate objects (He doesn't do that), but rather, I just began to notice the glory of who He is in every aspect of provisions over my life. I began to recognize how He provides for me in every moment with every experience, not just the dramatic ones.

I began to relax during those storms and found that I would more easily bend with the winds when they persisted. When I'm hot, He provides the breeze. When I'm thirsty, He provides the living water to refresh me. My mind is transformed!

I can see His grandeur in the tops of the trees where I look for Him, but also in the tiny birdhouse that hangs from the branch of the limb in my yard. He provides the chair that holds my body up as I rock back and forth. He's in the telephone that connects me to my family when I am physically far away from them. He kisses me in the wind on my face and checks in on me with a sweet smell of pine mountain air. He's warming me with the cup of coffee at my tableside and speaking through me in the keypad I am typing these words upon.

On days like today, when I want to run to be in solitude to contemplate how I will lead others up the mountains so they might get a better look at Him too, He laughs at me with thunder, then comforts me with the music of nature as I type.

[38]Sit with me awhile, and I'll share my glory with you through nature, He says. Each time I pick a scripture, He meets me there while simultaneously sending in a hummingbird to buzz over my balcony railing as if to say, "Because of Christ I see you, just share your love for me with others, and they will see me too." Then I would breath, relaxing into him again. With every misty breath, I would feel His reassurance that He is sharing Himself all-around me.

It does not matter if I run to the mountains or the beach; God has gone before me and surrounds me. He has purposed my every branch: dead ones, green ones, the bent, and the broken ones. He lives in my chaos and my quietness, in my contemplation and counting of moments, minutes, and miracles. He lives. He is not distant. He is ever near dancing with me in the ocean, pine, or plumeria scent of Him. If I allow Him, He will lift my eyes off myself and toward others climbing those mountains during a storm, trying to find Him as I once was. Storms can become time at God's hand where we learn to trust Him with intensity one season at a time.

---

[38] . *"But ask the animals, and they will teach you, or the birds in the sky, and they will tell you; 8 or speak to the earth, and it will teach you, or let the fish in the sea inform you. 9 Which of all these does not know that the hand of the LORD has done this? 10 In his hand is the life of every creature and the breath of all mankind. Job 12:7-10 NIV*

Chaos and Quietness

Seasons allow the process of His bigger picture to unfold. The Forest canopy of life, the tree, the branch, the leaf, the fruit, the seed, the root, the soil, the detail, and its grandeur. Through seasonal rhythms with Him, you don't fight. You simply grow. He isn't forcing but inviting you into every moment with Him. One season you may find the Holy Spirit leading you to your purpose. You might realize what God has called you to the following season is real and important work, and storms are just part of the plan.

Adding Hope, Faith, and Love to the soil of life is both complex and yet simple to do. Know you are not alone in your struggles. You are not the only one with the questions on your heart or chaos in your life. Feeling chaotic is how we "know" we are being offered an opportunity to grow. But we have to choose to add Christ's hope during times of chaos. It's the only way to see God's bigger purpose through it and find peace with it. You will have many opportunities to be fruitful in the future if you take the time now to do this hope-building work.

Remember, chaos is simply an opportunity to grow, and Spring is the perfect season to formulate a life-giving plan. Summer is just around the corner, and that is where you'll express yourself!

Are you ready for Summer?

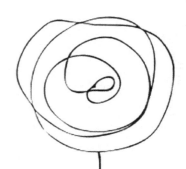

~Summer~

Chaos & Quietness of Summer

> Only God gives wisdom; he gives knowledge and understanding. He stores up wisdom for those who are honest. Like a shield he protects the innocent."
>
> Proverbs 2:6-7 NCV

Purpose / Expression

We've been metaphorically likening our seasonal journey of quieting chaos to the needs of a fruit-bearing tree, so think of Summer as a time where your previous season's blossoms begin fruiting in artistic symbolism of expressed energy. Trees of every shape and size with life-bearing potential can utilize the sun's natural lengthened energy cycles. But Summer is also a time of newfound strength, purpose, and expression, so I want to take you in a new direction with a metaphor related to energy and thirst.

Since Summer is a time for application and purposeful expression, let's start this chapter with this thought: Movement without wisdom is a waste of energy and can easily lead to a distracted, dehydrated state of being during a hot Summer season.

> **Staying hydrated with living water now will guide your movement toward divine assignments rather than pride objectives.**

The focused energy of a Summer season is gleaned from the lessons learned during our prior seasons. We've acquired wisdom and knowledge that will allow us to cleanse and let go of outcomes during Fall, how to rest and be comforted through Winter. While digging around in the soil of our Spring foundations, we've built up muscles of perseverance, resilience and formulated a hope-filled plan just in time for purposeful Summer application.

Everything about Summer communicates excitement. Summer's very first day holds the longest day of radiating light of the year as if the season is saying to us that God is going [39]before and behind, lighting the way, so get ready to move in complete confidence of where He is sending you! As Summer pushes the darkness back further and further into the evening, longer periods of pure light combine with energy to provide longer days of opportunity for this purposeful movement.

So, let's check in on the plans we've built in our previous season. You may find it helpful to stay here a while and hydrate on [40]living water while you review these purposeful questions that will help you clarify your Summer objectives.

---

[39] . *Before a word is on my tongue you, Lord, know it completely. You hem me in behind and before, and you lay your hand upon me. Such knowledge is too wonderful for me, too lofty for me to attain, Psalm 139;4-6*

[40] . *For the Lamb at the center of the throne will be their shepherd; 'he will lead them to springs of living water.' 'And God will wipe away every tear from their eyes.'" Revelation 7:17 NIV*

Chaos & Quietness Of Summer

Express Yourself

Before we launch into the activity of Summer's expression, let me ask you if you believe you are living out your purpose, or are you just living?

To live out your purpose, you have to move in agreement with the vision God wants to unleash within you and express through you. That agreement comes from a love for Christ and a love for others. Our Bible tells us [41]whatever we do, to work at it with all our heart as if working for the Lord, not for men, and that is living-waters wisdom. As God takes you through the season of your life, He gives you an understanding of the passions of your heart.

> **He put your specific passions, skills, abilities, strengths, and heartaches there because your life expression is meant to be unique to you yet created from His purpose, the Kingdom purpose for which you were born!**

Here is some really exciting news: All this expression begins and ends with love! When Jesus was challenged to summarize all the "to do's" of the Bible, His response was very clear. "Love the Lord God with all your heart and with all your soul and with all your mind and with all your strength. Then he said, Love your neighbor as yourself.' There is no commandment greater than these" (Mark 12:30-31).

---

[41] . *Whatever you do, work at it with all your heart, as working for the Lord, not for human masters, since you know that you will receive an inheritance from the Lord as a reward. It is the Lord Christ you are serving. Colossians 3:23-24*

Do you struggle with the idea or expression of love? There is an entire chapter about this subject in the New Testament (1 Corinthians 13). There are so many rewards for creating relationships on the principles and directives found in this chapter. These living water principles help us:

- Become patient with ourselves and others.
- Treat people with kindness and connect with people you don't feel the need to compete with.
- Be affirming to others and receive affirmation.
- Forgive and be forgiven.
- Live by and live in acceptance of one another.

Sounds dreamy, right! Well, it is possible to live in and live out a life of love. You simply have to accept the inexpressible grace of God and then trust Him to use your unique configuration of emotions, thoughts, character, potential, passions, and past lessons learned for His ultimate plan of expressing His love through us—Uniquely Us!

So let's look at some of the ways God has wired you to navigate life. The following questions may help you understand the unique ways in which you enjoy sharing love with others naturally. Past lessons, heartbreaks, chaos, storms, and painful experiences will be repurposed when you mix them with living water and share it.

Stop getting distracted and dehydrated by wondering who you are and what your purpose in life is. Instead, start moving in the direction of your specific calling in a way that only YOU were designed to do it. Follow the sound of living water through Scripture as you consider the answers to the following questions.

- What are some of the things you care most deeply about?

- Is there a specific group of people you have more influence over than another?
- Who might you be most interested in hanging around and serving?
- What kinds of needs can you meet right now? Physical, Spiritual, Mental, Emotional?
- What kinds of needs do you *enjoy* meeting and why?
- Have you learned some seasonal lessons that you could pass on to others?
- What causes you to become excited when you think about it?
- Is there a place, person, or project to which you would enjoy donating time, talent, or treasures?
- During the past Springs of your life, what actions steps have you considered but never moved on?

Some of this work may be part of your Spring planning cycles, while its summer expression is a natural byproduct of your understanding more clearly what it is. God will never give you abilities that aren't in line with your calling. But using your abilities, time, talents, and treasures for Christ will lead you to discover some extraordinary gifts God has planned for you to bless the body of believers with. You will never know what they are if you don't step out in faith to be used and useful to that Divine assignment!

I see Jesus as pure light and living water. My energy Creator. My love for Him allows me to race ahead during this Summer with purpose. Mind you; Summer energy expenditure will hold us true to our values. So, we best know our natural inclinations and how that helps or hinders us from living out our Divine assignments. So many times, I've had to stop mid-summer excitement, become teachable, and wait on God's timing before rushing ahead into another project or Summer plan. Summer kind of reveals the honesty of our relationship with Christ and with others. It's quite an exciting season to experience. There is so much energy to expend and so many choices we can make with our free will. But it's that thirst for Him that directs our steps and renews with joy and eternal purpose as we move.

Sunny Summer seasons are perfect for the consumption of juicy cooling foods literally found in abundance during Summer. It's God's way of physically providing for us during these hot and busy seasons, but be aware of taking on more than you can assimilate during Summer. The later the day gets, the lighter the meal, and the more fluid you should drink. Physically speaking, it's just better for your digestion and clear thinking. But metaphorically speaking, your life energy expenditure will either be guided by Money or the Living Water of Christ.

If you find yourself dehydrated and unclear, wandering and uncertain if you are trying to conform to what the world wants from you, you are probably chasing something as temporal as money.

> **Christ may provide you with a blessing of money so you may serve your purpose, but he will never require you to serve money to accomplish His will. You cannot serve two masters.**

If you're in an unpleasant job now, perhaps finding a way to live more simply may reduce the stress you feel to stay in a job or situation that is taking you away from living out your effectiveness for God. Twenty percent of the things on your to-do list probably "need" to be done. The other eighty percent should be time spent working out self-governing, moral objectives that help you make a more significant impact for Christ.

Your primary ministry may require several seasons of being home with your children or caring for your husband. There is no shame in having your priorities set on the things the world dismisses. Perhaps your household is your primary ministry for this season. Perhaps it is affirming sisters and brothers in the body. Whatever it is, just ask God to increase your effectiveness or open new doors that lead to fulfillment based on the unique way He has already impassioned you.

Summer chaos generally involves purposelessness, self-centered thought, and anything contrary to stability, security, courageous or grounded judgment, basically, lack of wisdom. Summer is the time to stick to the plans you made during Spring.

Remember, movement without wisdom is a waste of energy and only leads to dehydration.

Move-in the rhythm of the season but acknowledge your natural thirst for Christ. You are being a Jesus girl (or guy) running after Christ full speed now. That requires a continuous cool drenching in relationship with Him. Summer heat makes us sweat. Sweating is designed to cool us while making us thirsty. But don't reach for any old liquid to quench that summer thirst. That only leads to chaos. Living water is what you need to accomplish your goals and sustain you through the season. And Living water is never out of reach once you've discovered the source.

If Summer's energy has you choosing projects, productivity, and busyness over purposefulness, you're probably on your way to dehydration and a season of hot chaos.

Sneaks Up

A Summer season of chaos sneaks up on you like this. In the peak heat of a Summer's day, you are working on a project with people you feel you have a certain level of influence and are deeply invested in. You acknowledge a thirst arising in the back of your throat but ignore the sensation over and over again. There is a series of moments where the affirmation of man or the influence of peers keeps you pushing forward. Projects and busyness keep you from noticing you are now standing alone. Dehydrated "and" no longer impacting the people with whom God had granted you the most influence, your thinking becomes even more unclear. In prideful stubbornness, you may continue with your investment of time in this Summer project. All the while, Christ will call to you to return to His protective shadow and rehydrate in Him.

If you proceed to ignore the warning calls of dehydration, the movement of your body will continue to slow while the mind continues racing ahead. Eventually, you'll find yourself in such double-minded chaos that you are blind and unsure of yourself or of which way to turn. You hear the voice of reason, but you are stuck in a spiritually dehydrated state. You may endeavor to make your way toward the voice of reason you know so well, but you can become lost and unsure which way to move. Then self-medication arrives on the scene. As you begin reaching for all manner of drink and distraction, you become willing to consume anything to quench this painful, parched sensation growing within you. But anything you consume, other than living water, only dehydrates you further, leading you further away from what you need most. You are aware now that the joy of life is draining away from you.

> **You will have to admit the painful truth to yourself before it's too late. You've become a prideful consumer of experience rather than a vessel through which God can bless others.**

Nothing can satiate your thirst for a purposeful living but Him.

[42]Purposeful movement is essential now. You will continue losing a pint of precious bodily fluid with every day wandering away from Him. Living Water must be replenished to keep your body from poisoning itself with waste products of your own metabolism and mind. Every day lived without living water in the heat of summer chaos steals more and more energy. Once fatigue sets in and thoughts become unclear, unlubricated joints begin to ache as a warning to stop moving, but you don't stop. Life-giving oxygen gets more difficult to breathe into your lungs. Carbon dioxide release starts to slow with every precious breath, and you become more apathetic, unaware of the Hope leak that has you moving towards apathy.

But if you stay in this space, the heat will continue to grow in intensity until it consumes you entirely.

Your choices are to burn from within from the consuming heat of chaos or let Christ guide you back to where Living Water flows.

Follow the sound. I know you know it: Scripture, prayer, worship, and fellowship. God does the work of salvation within you, but you must move toward Him.

At this moment, God has your full attention.

Your mind races through the questions of "how" and begins to formulate the first utterances of "Help!"

- How did I end up here?
- Was I hyper-focused on a project or a goal without a good Spring plan?
- Did I slip away from God's protective grasp because I was over-focused on work and became less focused on giving God the glory for it?

---

[42] *"You use steel to sharpen steel, and one friend sharpens another" Proverbs 27:17 NIV*

- Did I miss the bigger picture of my effort?
- Did I forget my purpose?
- Did I ignore the early thirst pains altogether just to keep moving ahead?
- Did I get ahead of God?
- Did I go in a different direction than what God had purposed me to move in this season?
- Was I pushing and pursuing my own agenda?
- Was I fighting and winning battles God didn't ask me to fight for him?

A "yes" answer to any of these questions may be insightful lessons for how we find ourselves exhausted in chaotic spiritual silence.

Exhaustion is a joy stealer for sure. But, exhaustion can happen in any season. Perhaps you summered right through Fall, Winter, and Spring, mixing your seasons, creating chaos upon chaos for each season with your tenacity.

Blind, [43]thirsty, alone, [44]exhausted. You still have a [45]choice in this chaos. Remember, chaos is neither good nor bad. It is neutral. What you do or don't do now makes chaos work for or against you.

As you humble yourself, calling out to Jesus, let Him refresh and restore you with Living Water. Crawl if you have to but

---

[43] .You desire but do not have, so you kill. You covet but you cannot get what you want, so you quarrel and fight. You do not have because you do not ask God. James 4:2 NIV

[44] . When you ask, you do not receive, because you ask with wrong motives, that you may spend what you get on your pleasures. James 4:3 NIV

[45] . Come near to God and he will come near to you. Wash your hands, you sinners, and purify your hearts, you double-minded. James 4:8 NIV

keep moving toward the sounds of rippling water. It's still there. It's always been there. The familiar sound just became silent to your mind for the familiarity of it. But it's right there and has been all along.

Your ministry and your movement matter to God. The best nourishment for your mind, body, and soul is God's Word. Drop to your knees, drink. Drink. Don't worry about moving from here. [46]Just drink. God is omniscient. He knows what we need before we even ask, but prayer is the means He uses to bring about the response. That prayer of "Help me Jesus" is all it takes to quench your thirst for life. Dwell here awhile. Feel the cool protection of the [47]shadow of the all-mighty Himself. Drink and regain purpose for living—purpose for life. With Living Water surging through you, you are free to move in the height of the Summer heat, fully protected by the shadow that saves your life and directs your steps. He will make you even stronger and more courageous than before.

Summer chaos reminds us to never again move out from under His protective covering. Your Summer's chaos can be repurposed, and activity can be restored. A guided, guarded, gifted, and grace-filled tempo ensues, but only when you're ready. Go only where He leads and run with confidant passion where He sends you. From here, just a few months ahead, Fall will remind us once again to let go of Summer's outcomes.

The Summers ahead may be getting hotter, but you will never become dehydrated and will forever move on purpose with

---

[46] . *Humble yourselves before the Lord, and he will lift you up. James 4:10 NIV*

[47] . *Whoever dwells in the shelter of the Most High will rest in the shadow of the Almighty*

Psalm 91:1

Christ. So continue in your journey now with confidence.[48] God will continue the good work He has started in you! Dedicating yourself to His Glory will give you the courage to move in ways you never thought possible. You are His masterpiece!

Story Time

A personal story of courage and vanity.

I'm insecure. There I said it out loud. I hate the word so much. I hide from it because somewhere along the line, I was told only perfection is good enough. In a way, that statement is true, but not the way I seemed to apply it to myself for most of my life. It wasn't until my late 30's that I discovered the perfection of my spirit, which comes through a perfect Christ, is the only correct application of perfection. However, like many women in today's society, I want to be one of the beautiful people. Now I rarely admit that to myself, yet I've put so much energy into obtaining it. So there, I said that out loud too.

But the moment I take my eyes off of the perfect God that is my Creator and start critiquing the way I was created, well, that just stirs up all kinds of immobilizing irrational self-loathing. I now realize I can't just be only the good parts of everyone I know and see, and I've learned to be more strategic about the energy I put into hiding my imperfections from the world. Through the wisdom drawn out of seasons and cycles of chaos, I've come to realize how perfectly imperfect this world is because of sin.

---

[48] *"...being confident of this, that he who began a good work in you will carry it on to completion until the day of Christ Jesus." Philippians 1:6 NIV*

Broken people fit perfectly into an imperfect world. But we were created for so much more than imperfect sin.

That gave me the freedom to move about this world with confidence in my imperfections because the only person I've learned to care about seeing me as perfect is God. And before Him, I can hide nothing. So I have a perfect Savior, Jesus, to cover over all the yucky parts and present me as perfect before God. Yup, Jesus does that. The more I came to learn and love Jesus, the less worried I became about how I fit into a broken world.

Today I'm much more interested in learning how to live as the blessed creation I was made to be in His image. But it's still one season of living and learning at a time, and God will turn up the heat wherever I'm deceiving myself!

Several summers ago, I'd been struggling through a cleansing cycle of self-esteem. But, unfortunately, I hadn't been able to let it go through a Fall pruning, nor had I found comfort through a Winter's rest or process it through the hope of Spring. So here I was, literally mid-summer in Mexico with my husband and a few good friends, poolside on vacation, hanging on to a poor body image.

I should have been enjoying the sun and surf, but instead, I was wrestling with the chaos in my head and dying of thirst in the hot summer sun. I'd chosen a location at the south end of the pool, farthest from the snack bar. The hot stone path around the pool was made even hotter by the rising temperature. It seemed everyone in the building was congregating around the pool's edge and my only option to reach the snack bar was to move past this massive crowd. I sat up briefly in my chair, to sum up the effort required for me to reach the bar. Just then, a tall butt-string bikini was making her way along the pebbled stone path. The onlookers (self-included) were captivated by her perfect form and the elegant confidence in which she moved, right up to the point where howls and hollers of various languages were spewed from all areas of the pool, all vying for her attention.

I just sat back in my chair. No longer appreciating her beauty and almost feeling violated by it, jealous of it, I lay in my lounge chair dying of thirst, thinking God was clearly not acting on my behalf when he made me the exact opposite of that elegant creature on the move at the pool. *Doing nothing is better than doing something to quench my thirst*, I tried to convince myself as I lay there in my self-loathing. *I can't possibly walk in her path. Everything about me jiggles.*

No, I'm serious! I'm holding myself to a ridiculous standard for a middle-aged woman, but it is an issue God has been pruning from me for years. Who doesn't want to feel at home in their own skin? Beauty is the crowning essence of a woman, or so I told myself. And at that moment, I felt anything but beautiful, so I took a deep breath in and let it out as I tried to quiet the chaos in my head and the growing thirst in my throat, and the chaos of that quietness.

I was momentarily distracted by my sandals and realized they didn't match my cover-up. Oh, the horror! I know. Don't laugh, but it was a real thing at the time. Somehow, I developed this theory that pretty matching sandals that go with earrings that match a bathing-suit cover-up might take the focus off my body imperfections should I be required to move around the pool. The preparation that went into a bathing suit trip took almost as long as the vacation lasted itself.

I surmised that all this "stuff" would somehow hide the way I felt about myself. Yet, there I lay, dying of thirst, now fretting over the wrong cover-up for my sandals and the wrong sandals for my earrings and feeling miserable about it all.

For this trip, I even pre-tanned myself with chemicals to lessen the appearance of the cellulite that seemed to be making its way to a new area of my body each season. I should have been enjoying the beautiful poolside, beachfront ocean view, but I had let the Enemy of my soul speak lies to me in the area I was most insecure about. I wanted to be sipping a wonderfully refreshing drink and not giving a crap about what other people thought of my body. I wanted to walk across that pool as confidently as she did. But instead, I sat there paralyzed in my foolishness. On that day, I had even managed to pick a suit that said "look at me," yet I really didn't want to be seen at all.

I'll never be one of those "beautiful people."

As the morning shifted to noon, the temperature had to have risen to 95 degrees. I felt a breeze cool my irritability just a little. I had to figure out how to work up the courage to put on my sandals and sarong and just go for it before I passed out in that humidity.

Why God! Why can't you just take away this insecurity! I was embarrassed by my own thought process and felt foolish by my lack of strength. I just didn't understand what was triggering those pieces of my unhealed heart. I was wrestling with a twisted view of who I was.

Finally, I worked up the courage to sit up in my chair and scan the pool. As I sat up, I noticed a streak of orange running down my right arm and dripping onto the white beach chair beneath me that also had an orange-colored outline of my body thanks to that self-tanner.

Could this day get any worse? I sighed.

My options were to sit there and sweat orange while waiting for one of the pool attendants to come over or get up and move.

About 50 feet away, I saw my husband emerging from the ocean, wet and cool looking. I thought for a moment about heading south to the water and avoid the pool area altogether. I could rinse my orange off in the ocean that way. But then I still had to walk past all the people on the beach, so I sat. I didn't move. I watch how others have mastered their life's movement, yet there I sat in shame, pulled down into that chair by my own misjudgment.

I watch Kevin walk towards me and towel off, shaking his full, organic head of soft grey hair into his towel, not a self-aware care in the world. His insecurities seem to be of a different kind.

He catches me looking at him:

"Why are you looking at me like I'm a Martian," he said, smiling down at me, a broad grin on his wet face.

"I just think you're so lucky not to be a girl. I mean, I'm grateful you are a guy and all, but if you spent one day in my body..." I say sarcastically.

"Whoa! You can just stop right there. If I spent one day in your body, I'd have to think with your head, and that is not a task I'm up for... ever." He adds, kissing me on the forehead before adjusting his towel into his beach chair and plopping atop of it.

"Well, spending a day in your head would be no picnic for me either, you know." I quirk back, causing him to raise an eyebrow at me to say he disagrees, but something stops him from engaging me. I'm guessing it was wisdom, having been married to me so many years now.

I sigh and slump back in my chair, still dying of thirst and hating myself for hating myself so much.

"Hey. Want something to drink?" He suddenly quips.

"Do I!" I respond.

"Well, why didn't you say something, honey. Here, I have some pesos in my bag. While you're up there, would you mind ordering me a sandwich with fries? I'm starving."

I just stare at him for a moment in silence, trying to decide if I want to cry or laugh. After what felt like an eternity between the two of us just staring at one another, neither one saying a word, I finally admitted to him that I didn't want to walk past all those people in my bathing suit. All he could do was contort the side of his face with a quint and say, "Why?"

"I just don't feel pretty today," I said quietly, embarrassed by my own admission.

"Don't be ridiculous, honey. You're beautiful." He says, half relieved and with a smile. "I don't know why you're so hard on yourself. I wish there were something I could say or do to help you understand that. You spend so much time and energy helping other women feel beautiful inside and out. I don't know why you can't you do that for yourself?"

Shrugging my shoulders, I offer up an "I really don't know" kind of look. "I honestly wish I could feel different in my body. I pray about it, and honestly, I know that at some point, I just have to do something different until I feel different."

"I think you need to have a little patience with yourself too. But honestly, honey, what's the worst thing that could happen if you just didn't care about what people thought. It doesn't make you a bad person. You're just not wired to be a selfish person, so you can take a little latitude on not giving a flip for a change. Just stop caring about what other people think about you and just focus on caring about other people. It's what you do best anyway," he said with a wink.

Those words were some of the most powerful words ever spoken over me. They helped me take the focus off of my self-loathing and apply a loving filter of service over my insecurity. I decided to move.

It suddenly seemed easier to walk up to that snack bar out of service to my husband than for my own thirst. God was using my heart of love for Kevin to show me how to love myself.

> **Healing will often come as a rescue mission amid our chaos.**

Jesus will thwart our self-healing attempts at hiding and replace it with his promise to destroy the grip of captivity the Enemy has on us. We are only a prisoner if we choose to be. My husband's voice reminded me of where my real beauty was cultivated from. Service.

"Okay fine. I'll go get you your sandwich and me something to drink," I say, standing up from my beach chair. "Only because I love you so much," I added as I reached over and grabbed my sarong and fastened it around my waist with confidence.

I took in a great gulp of courage, and I grabbed those pesos from my husband's hand and slipped my feet into my un-matching sandals. "Well, here I go!"

Nothing had changed except my mindset, and I suspect something deep within my heart had healed, if just slightly through Kevin's life-giving words. I made my way up the stairs toward the pool bar.

Halfway across the pool path, I hear a cat-whistle. It's my husband making a scene from clear across the pool in an attempt to help me laugh at myself. And I did. I smiled, blew him a kiss, and waved. Of course, parts of my arm continued waving well after I'd stopped, but at that moment, I was okay with that too.

I continued my leisurely walk toward the pool bar and decided to keep the smile that my hubby had placed on my face. As I was walking, I was smiling at guests along my route. I offered a "Buenos tardes" here and there and received smile after smile in return. Once to the pool bar, I ordered my drink and my hubby's meal. I enjoyed a few moments of pleasant conversation at the bar and had utterly forgotten my insecurity, at least for the moment.

Once the food was ready, and my thirst was quenched, I began the walk back across the pool to where my husband was waiting. I had found a new freedom by making an effort to do something different with all that Summer energy. I let my true beauty radiate by allowing my heart to be tended, seen, heard, and healed.

I still struggle with deep childhood wounds of insecurity that may never completely dissipate, but I refuse to be held captive and immobilized by fear or self-loathing any longer! I am ready to *move through the chaos with purpose*.

This is the Summer of my life!

So let me ask you; are you ready to quiet your chaos and find the chaos that is stealing your quietness with God, yourself, and others?

This is the Summer of our lives, friends.

Let us move with purpose as we trust Jesus' Word.

He came to [49]seek, save, and restore!

So let me ask you again—Are you ready!

Well then, Let's Go!

---

[49] *"For the Son of Man came to seek and to save the lost." Luke 19:10 NIV*

The Invitation

I love being a Jesus girl because I can relate to Christ's chaos. So walk with me a moment here, and let's take a look at His story of chaos from birth to baptism. It's a story of hope that starts with disbelief.

His birthing circumstances were quite chaotic. First, there was the whole messy manger situation and Mary having to travel on the back of a donkey while eight months pregnant. Yikes! Then His story moves into a chaotic reception by the people He was called to love, and all the babies of His time were ordered to be killed because of His birth. Later, as He tried to reach out to them to teach them love as an adult, He was tortured in return. Eventually, He was mocked and strung up on a cross, rejected by the weight of sin He took to that cross with Him for our sake. Such chaos surrounded His life—And then came death. That would be a considerably chaotic ending if that were all there was to the chaos (and I skipped a few seasons too).

But something inspiring happens through all that chaos, and it happened to the heart of humanity. There is a spirit of hope being birthed amongst courageous believers right at a time it seems all hope is lost. God had always been speaking through the chaos to our messy humanity with the Good News of Jesus overcoming the ultimate chaos itself, which is... Death.

God's grace-filled gift to messy, chaotic humanity is victory over death! I mean, what's the worst thing that could happen to me today? Does chaos kill me? But if that's the worst, and my hope is in Christ, even the worst isn't the end of my hope. See, we get to live life "to the fullest" with Him in this complicated, messy, chaotic life and the perfect next life! Thus, His and our unpleasant chaos ends up in an eternal triumph over death and an eternal victory of hope for you and me.

I interviewed many believers and non-believers for this book. For most believers, chaos seemed to be a time of renewal and opportunity for strengthening and rediscovery of faith. For a few fence-sitters, chaos was a hope-stealer and thief. But every single indifferent non-believer said almost the same thing: that the knowledge chaos brought them about their own limitations left them defeated, hopeless, and even more lost after the chaos than before it.

The one thing most everyone had in common was that their stories of chaos were well guarded and deeply personal experiences, and each chaotic season left each of them forever changed one way or another.

No, I didn't always choose hope in the chaos of the early years of my life, but that's where the really good stories of hope come alive for me now. I'm at a season where Scripture has proven to me, beyond any doubt, that no matter how messy my chaos is, or how alone in it I may feel, it is a theological impossibility for chaos itself to separate me (or you) from God if you choose Him over your chaos. In fact, chaos was most often used to point me back to a deeper faith in Christ.

So, if you want to receive Christ's peace, here is a personal invitation.

Receiving Christ involves an act of our free will. A Christ-directed life is one where you put Christ in charge of your life, and you yield (surrender) to Him. That means your interests, plans, and actions are going to be directed and repurposed by Christ, resulting in harmony with God's plan and harmony even during your chaos.

You can receive Christ right now by faith through prayer. Prayer is just talking with God. He knows your heart, so don't worry about getting your words just right. Just talk to Him. Read the following suggested prayer, and if it expresses the desire of your heart, Christ will come into your life as promised.

"Lord Jesus, I want to know you personally. Thank you for dying on the cross for my sins. I open the door of my life and receive you as my Savior and Lord. Thank you for forgiving me of my sins and giving me eternal life. Take control of my life. Make me the kind of person You want me to be."

If you have done this, then congratulations! Luke 15:7 says that when one sinner accepts Jesus Christ as their Savior, the angels rejoice, so there's a party going on in Heaven right now over your decision!

The Bible promises eternal life to all who receive Christ:

"God has given us eternal life, and this life is in his Son. He who has the Son has the life; he who does not have the Son of God does not have the life. I write these things to you who believe in the name of the Son of God so that you may know that you have eternal life" (1 John 5:11-13).

Now, thank God often that Christ is in your life and that He will never leave you. May I suggest you look into reading Scripture to sustain you? If you've never read the Bible before, I always recommend starting in the New Testament: Matthew, Mark, Luke, then John. It will seem like you are reading the same story four times, and well, you are. You are just reading it from four different perspectives written to four different groups of people at the time. But once you understand Jesus, you can more easily understand how the impossible becomes possible throughout the rest of Scripture.

> **If Christ lives in you, you have eternal life from the very moment you invited Him in, and that, my friend, is the surprisingly simple truth behind finding the quietness in your chaos and understanding the chaos that is stealing your quietness with Christ.**

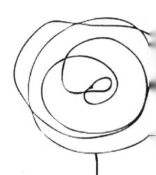

Dedication

For Jesus and all He has called to rest in him or return to Him. May we always serve well together in His name.

To my rock, my husband Kevin. You are my forever hero. Thank you for all the things that you *don't do*, that assure me of your love. I am blessed that you would allow yourself to be the vessel through which God has abundantly blessed my heart from the day we met. Every year I find more reasons to love you with confidence until the end of time.

To my daughter, Amber-Mae. You have made my life worth living from the moment God gave you breath. I see this incredible strength and courage that radiates God's loving truths through you. You are capable of anything you put your mind to. You are wildly entertaining and your mind is amazing. I just really like you! I have raised you to be a warrior woman and that solid love you have for Christ brings me more joy than you could possibly know. Thank you for honoring me as your momma through all the seasons. You are forever deeply appreciated, admired, respected, cherished and loved.

Dedication

To my first grandchild, my sweet Sadie'Mae. You fill me with joy and bring me hope for all tomorrows with every precious snuggle. To experience such joy bubbling out of you for Jesus at such a young age is inspiring. God made you special for a reason. He has BIG plans for you, little button. Keep your eyes focused on Him no matter the storms that come your way because you are a joy-bringer of light into any chaotic season. You are now and will forever be my sunshine. You are unique, perfect, and capable of anything in Him! I'm so lucky I get to be your Mae'me! I love you deeply.

To my second born grandchild, Ryker James. You bring me the pleasures of a new kind of chaotic rest and recovered strength. I adore your warm hugs and those sparkling blue eyes pierce right to my heart. God created a special blend of tenderness and toughness in you, my little redheaded firefly. You are gifted to find solutions to situations that others miss, and in Christ's strength you are a great warrior for good. Give that Summer fire of yours to God, and He will do amazing things with it, my love. This Mae'me loves you sweetly, permanently, and forever, my little angel!

To Ryan, my son-in-law. Your life is an incredible story of God's love. Your walk of faith and unwavering dedication to your family and self-development is solid and inspiring. You are brilliant, tender, and not to be messed with. I adore that in you. You are a great blessing to this Mommas heart. I love you.

To Harrison my stepson, my son. You are a brilliant man. I enjoy the way you crash the brick walls of education in order to reach your goals. Your viewpoint on life inspires me to be a better person. You will always be a special part of my daily prayers. May you discover for yourself the beauty of the quieting of the chaos in your life through Christ's love. You are loved and prayed over daily and always.

For Dawn, my first grammatical editor. Thank you for your hours of dedication to this project as an act of love. Your belief in me and words of wisdom that "God would not provide my next ministry until I finished this one" was the catalyst to completing what I started so long ago through this book. Thank you for your friendship. Thank you for the encouragement that I could make a difference with story.

For my two besties, Rocio and Tina, and all the students, pastors, friends and family who inspire me daily through their own chaotic walks. I thank you for always loving me as I am.

I thank God for you all.

About the Author

Cynthia Hartson Ross is a lover of God's Word, Prayer Warring Grandma of two, inspirational conference speaker, writer, natural health care authority, retired esthetician and forever an entrepreneur.

As a contracted staff member and longtime core volunteer for a California-based mega church, she was part of their first church plant team to develop a campus model that is now utilized globally. She reflects on those ministry years as some of the most chaotic, fruit-filled, character-revealing years of her life.

In 2019, Cynthia entered a season of leadership rest to pursue more time with her two grandchildren, Ryker and Sadie'Mae. She writes from the heart and speaks to inspire. As a natural entrepreneur, having owned and operated a variety of natural health and beauty businesses, she is staying connected to the industry as a brand representative for a home-based skin, hair, and wellness care company while enjoying the idea of ministering through writing.

"Each season of quiet and chaos reassures me that God can use my questionable writing skills for His glory and for your peace." ~Cynthia Ross

CPSIA information can be obtained
at www.ICGtesting.com
Printed in the USA
LVHW051244161121
703482LV00010B/638